G.....
TO GOD

LESSONS MY
DAD TAUGHT ME

SHELLY GARLOCK HAMILTON

CONTENTS

FOREWORD

Frank Watson Garlock was the man Randy, Gina, and I were privileged to call "Dad." He was born on August 10, 1930, to Edward Arthur and Alice Mae Garlock. He grew up in the small township of Montclair, New Jersey and was fourth in line of nine children.

Our father's family was poor in material goods but rich in love. His poverty left him not feeling entitled but choosing to work hard instead. Dad was rich because he was fortunate to be part of a loving family. Most importantly, from a young age, Dad exhibited a tender heart toward God.

The life of a godly father is one of the greatest gifts a child can acquire. In retrospect, lessons from fathers help shape the minds and lives of the children fortunate enough to receive them. When I think back on the life of my dad, many of the lessons he taught me were more caught than taught. Frank Garlock was a good man, and I loved him with all my heart.

God admonishes fathers everywhere to "teach [the words of Scripture] diligently unto thy children, and shalt talk of them when thou sittest in thine house, and when thou walkest by the way, and when thou liest down, and when thou risest up" (Deuteronomy 6:7).

Lessons My Dad Taught Me is a book born out of a heart that desires to share the character-developing and life-changing lessons our dad instilled in Randy, Gina, and me. I want to mention that we as a family make no claim that our dad was perfect. His love for us, however, was unmistakable, entrenched and enriched in God's love. Through ups and downs, Dad's unfailing love was the glue that held our family together.

One of the most influential puzzle pieces in a child's life is the presence of and interaction with a father. Hopefully, an earthly father will give the impression, though flawed at best, of the mercy and love of our heavenly Father. Though undeserved, this was the example Dad left for me.

At the outset of this book, I feel it important that you, the reader, are made aware of Dad's brilliant mind. Our family believes Dad had what is referred to as an eidetic memory. He remembered most people he'd met and things he'd done along with precise time frames. Dad could memorize the intricate scores of operas he conducted. His incredible memory was a gift from God that proved to enhance all he did in his lifetime. His sharp mind—his accurate recollection, biblical knowledge, and wisdom—was the rich resource which made this book possible.

As many daughters are, I am and will always be a "Daddy's girl." People would often tell Dad and me that we looked alike. Dad always responded with, "But on her it looks good."

Frank Garlock was an amazing man—a man I took pride in calling Daddy.

I love you, Daddy.

Always, Shelly

1 DAD TAUGHT ME TO
"GIVE IT TO GOD"

> *Humble yourselves therefore under the mighty hand*
> *of God, that he may exalt you in due time: Casting*
> *all your care upon him; for he careth for you.*
> *—1 Peter 5: 6-7*

In Dad's final days, my sister Gina asked him, "Dad, what is the greatest lesson your life taught you—something you'd like people to know?" Without hesitation, Dad replied, "Give it to God." Gina asked him to explain further. Dad said, "Give God everything—your life, your time, your money, your talents. Everything." Dad later added, "—And see what amazing things He does."

Dad had confidence that He could give everything to God because he had a firm belief in God's goodness. Dad saw it everywhere. He saw God's creation—His bringing mankind into existence, His caring for the smallest sparrow, and in His painting flowers and butterflies with beautiful colors—as proof: God is good.

God created man as a sensory being. God is the originator and author of happiness, fulfillment, fellowship, enjoyment, and pleasure. Food tastes good, flowers smell fragrant, and fun is fun because of God. In fact, God promises all the same pleasurable and good things in heaven—but in abundance. Who wouldn't want to give everything to this good God?

Just as anything good comes from God, anything that isn't, doesn't. Satan is the author of sin, sickness, sorrow, and death. Satan wants us to believe that bad things happen because God is not good, but it is instead, because Satan is evil.

God's goodness was ultimately displayed in sending His only Son, Jesus Christ, to leave the comforts of heaven, come to this sin-ridden world, and die a horrible death on the cross, so that mankind could be saved from his sin. This sacrificial act was also due to God's goodness.

Dad didn't believe that God was good because his life was hardship free. In fact, I think Dad's life actually had more sorrows, disappointments, and challenges than most. His older sister was committed to a mental hospital when he was a teen. His youngest brother lost his arm in a tragic paper mill accident. In Dad's twenties, his middle brother died due to alcoholism. And Dad lost his younger sister due to a brain tumor.

When Ron's and my son, Jonathan, became ill with schizophrenia,

Dad suffered greatly. Jonathan was his oldest grandchild. Dad also lived through his wife, Flora Jean's dementia as well as my husband, Ron's.

Dad spoke often about adumbrations—short concise phrases that represent and help visualize something, often as a type of foreshadowing. "Give it to God" is a perfect example of an adumbration.

In my opinion, it is one of the last, yet greatest pearls of wisdom Dad left. I consider it to be his legacy to pass on to my children, theirs, and generations to come. Dad's voice reiterating "Give it to God" on his deathbed, comes constantly to mind as I am left to finish my life's race without him.

My desire is that you, if you have not, will also be convinced in your own heart that God is good and that you as well can "give it to God."

2 DAD TAUGHT ME
WHEN YOU LEAVE GOD OUT, NOTHING MAKES SENSE

> *In the beginning God created the heaven and the earth.* —Genesis 1:1

Through the annals of time, the world has tried to leave God out. Dad and I would be listening to scientists tout their theories of evolution or watching some of the foolishness of liberal politician's ideologies when Dad would say, "When you leave God out, nothing makes sense."

How many theories have scientists come up with to try and explain creation, leaving God out? Evolutionists claim that each of the different creation theories they have espoused follows "the science." What is it: Darwin's theory of natural selection, the theory of mutation, the Big Bang theory, or the modern synthetic theory? All these theories have logical holes and cannot be duplicated or observed. Many of their "so-called proofs" can be explained by the biblical account of a worldwide flood.

Evolutionist's atheistic "science" constantly changes regarding the origin of the universe. Dad would tell me, "Science constantly evolves while God remains constant." For instance, scientists have recently reported that the world is twenty-six billion years old rather than the previously thought thirteen billion. When you leave God out, not only does nothing makes sense but the "nothing" becomes foolish and ridiculous.

The biblical account of creation has always indicated a young earth, confirmed by the number of "age rings" in the oldest tree known and by the living matter discovered inside excavated dinosaur bones—only possible with a young earth.

Dad was particularly concerned about all the lies told by experts regarding the 2020 COVID pandemic and its origins. God cannot be and is not a part of untruth and fearmongering. We are now told that the COVID deaths reported at the time were as much as 50 percent exaggerated. Because God was left out, fear and lies took over, causing deceptive reports and poor decisions affecting everyone: women gave birth without their husband's presence, loved ones died alone in assisted living facilities, vaccinations were often unnecessary, children were denied hands-on education and community, and suicides were rampant all over the world.

What makes more sense than God? The Apostle John in the New Testament coincides with Genesis, "All things were made by him [God]; and without him was not any thing made that was made" (John 1:3). Common sense concurs with Genesis and John. No one would believe that a manufactured watch came into existence by a big bang, with all the intricate parts randomly flying together, fitting perfectly, and—*voilà*—the time of day inexplicably appears.

In converse to the world leaving God out, when God is included, everything makes sense. Even each person's unique DNA gives testament to the hands-on involvement of an all-wise Maker.

Dad, you were right. When you leave God out, nothing makes sense.

3 DAD TAUGHT ME TO
BE CONTENT WITH LITTLE OR MUCH

> *Not that I speak in respect of want: for I have learned, in whatsoever state I am, therewith to be content.* —Philippians 4:11

As previously stated, the Edward Garlock family was extremely poor. The family consisted of three adults and nine children: Alice (my grandma), Edward (my grandpa), Vic (my great uncle, a retired World War II veteran who lived with the family), seven boys, and two girls.

When Dad was a young child, his family lived in a small three-bedroom rented home. Dad and three of his brothers slept in what amounted to an overgrown closet. This makeshift "room" contained a full-sized bed and a set of bunkbeds that stuck out into the hallway. The mattress Dad slept on with his brother Bob was so old and worn, that no matter where Dad and Bob started out, they both ended up sunk in the middle.

The Garlock children ate oatmeal for breakfast with canned milk. They were then bussed to the Verona Women's League Club where they received a hot lunch tray which included a vitamin tablet. For supper they ate Corn Flakes with evaporated milk mixed with water.

There were concerned citizens from the city of Verona that looked out for poor kids. The Verona Women's League not only fed poor children a hot lunch but also sent them to summer camp. Going to camp was great, but the league didn't think to send Dad and his siblings with any spending money. When the other kids would buy ice cream or go to the craft shop, Dad and his siblings could not. He vowed that if he was ever able to support kids to go to camp, he would also send them with a little spending money.

Some of Dad's siblings became bitter due to their family being poor. In contrast, Dad learned to work hard and remain content. I believe God blessed Dad due to his becoming a victor and not a victim despite his lack of material goods.

Because of Dad's upbringing, whatever ministry Dad became a part of, he did not ask how much his salary would be. He always figured that if God led him to a certain place, God would take care of him and his family.

My siblings and I didn't even realize when we had little because Daddy was never anything but cheerful. Because of my dad's attitude, our family was content wherever we lived—whether the second story over a church gym or a three-room, pre-owned army bunker on the Bob Jones University (BJU) campus.

Mom, too, shared Dad's sentiments. She, Flora Jean, grew up on a small farm in Oklahoma. Although her dad owned many farmlands, their family lived a simple life. Mom even learned to make her own clothes.

Because of Mom and Dad's humble beginnings, even though later in life they could afford nicer things, they never forgot their roots. I was, therefore, taught to be content with little or much.

4 DAD TAUGHT ME
KINDNESS UPSTAGES TALENT

> *Let no corrupt communication proceed out of your*
> *mouth, but that which is good to the use of edifying,*
> *that it may minister grace unto the hearers. . . . And*
> *be ye kind one to another, tenderhearted.*
> *—Ephesians 4:29, 32*

Dad was a talented musician. As a teenager, Dad sang with the Roseville Singers from New Jersey. Once, when the choir performed an a cappella concert in The Townhall of New York City, Dad was responsible for humming the next song's starting pitch for the singers. He could do this by ear, without the aid of a pitch pipe or keyboard.

Dad was a talented trombonist. Several of The New York Philharmonic Symphony trombonists heard Dad play when he was thirteen. He had been first chair in the New Jersey Allstate orchestra and could play in any clef, even when the clef changed in the middle of a scale passage of sixteenth notes.

Because these musicians saw Dad's potential for greatness, they let him sit in on their symphony rehearsals. This enabled Dad to play under famous conductors/composers such as Aaron Copeland, Morton Gould, and Leroy Anderson. When it was time for Dad to go to college, the symphony trombonists got Dad a scholarship to Julliard, thinking he would someday take one of their places. Dad also received an appointment to get a scholarship to West Point by a local New Jersey senator.

However, before Dad made a decision, he had one more opportunity presented to him. Elmer Piper, uncle of author John Piper, heard Dad play his trombone at an evangelistic meeting. Afterwards, Mr. Piper told Dad's mother, Alice, that BJU might be a good choice for Dad's schooling. Dad felt that Elmer Piper's recommendation, a school where he could receive Bible as well as musical training, would be God's best choice for him.

When Dad told the New York Symphony friends of his decision to go to BJU, they got mad and said, "You don't know what you are giving up. You're going to be sorry." Dad told me, "But I never was." All of Dad's talent could have led him in a completely different direction from ministry. But Dad had a tender heart to serve God, wherever that led him.

Dad had known of talented young men that didn't stay in ministry because they never learned how to minister to and serve others. Their talent puffed them up to be bigger than their britches. Dad taught me, "Being kind is preferable to talent. It is easier to learn musical skills than people skills."

Being kind when working with people is critical in any ministry. When a problem would come up in our church, Dad would joke, "I'd have a great ministry, if it weren't for people."

I must add that the blessing of talent is not to be underestimated. Dad could have been one of the trombonists in the New York Philharmonic Symphony Orchestra or a great conductor in the world's eyes. Dad's decision to instead go into the Lord's service shows a heart not haughty, but tender to serve God and others. Kindness always upstages talent.

5 DAD TAUGHT ME
FAITH OVERCOMES FEAR

> The just shall live by faith. —Romans 1:17

Dad's Grandma, Sadie Campbell Laird, was a dedicated Christian and a great soul winner. While living for a time in Sebring, Florida due to her husband's health, she had the privilege to win Elma Cook to the Lord.

Elma had been the nurse of Charles Cook and later became his wife. He, though crippled, became a great inventor. The book *The Genius Who Never Walked a Step* was written about Charles Cook's inventions for train and steamboat engines that are still in use today.

Elma called my great grandmother, "Mrs. Sadie," and referred to her as her spiritual mother. I am blessed to have the Bible Dad's Grandma Sadie gifted him, given to her by Elma Cook.

When Dad decided to go to college at BJU, he was penniless. Dad's oldest brother Ed gave him the money he had received from serving in the Marines. With it, Dad was able to buy a train ticket on the Silver Meteor to get him to Greenville, South Carolina.

Dad arrived at Bob Jones in January of 1949, the second semester of the school year.

The money left over after the train ticket was purchased, bought Dad's textbooks with only two pennies left over. (Those same two pennies remained in his pants pocket at the end of his freshman year.)

Dad bravely got into the registration line, knowing he had no money left to pay for tuition or room and board. He had total faith that God wanted him there and would work out the financial details. He was hoping he could get a job and pay his way through. When he got in line, he was asked, "What's your name?"

Dad was afraid to say, so he said instead, "I know I don't have the first month's tuition, but I can work. If you will just give me a job." Dad was cut off with, "Ok, tell me your name?" He continued, "I can work wherever—" "Just give me your name."

Dad finally answered, "Frank Garlock." As she found his name on the registration list, she responded with, "Your first month tuition is paid." Thinking she hadn't heard him right, Dad replied again, "My *name* is Frank Garlock."

Although Dad was not aware at the time, his Grandma Sadie had proudly told a certain Mrs. Cook about Dad's studying to be a preacher. As a favor to his grandma, and certainly as an offering to the Lord, Elma Cook paid his entire way through BJU, one month at a time—never late, never in advance. Also, a man named Mel Hunter was burdened to help by mailing Dad toiletries and school supplies.

Choosing faith over the fancy scholarship set the destiny of Dad's life. Faith overcomes fear and leads you to the best places.

6 DAD TAUGHT ME
TO BE TENACIOUS

> *Finally, my brethren, be strong in the Lord, and in the power of his might. — Ephesians 6:10*

Dad figured that because God had provided his tuition, and he didn't need to get a job at BJU to pay for it, he would use every spare minute to give his time back to God. He spent his weekends in some sort of ministry. For instance, his first semester, Dad was invited to join several young men doing chapel services for Greenville's homeless by playing his trombone and leading songs.

During the school week at Bob Jones, Dad was formally developing his music ministry skills in music classes. But he was also watching and learning by imitation. During BJU chapel services, the song leader, Herbert Hoover, made the congregation follow him and do musical things. Dad watched closely and tried to imitate him when he himself led singing. For some reason, Dad thought memorizing books of jokes would also help his song leading ministry as well. As a side note, Dad learned so many jokes that he was asked to girl's dating outings just to be the emcee. If the food arrived late, Dad could fill the time entertaining everyone.

After Dad's freshman year, Elma Cook told his grandma, Mrs. Sadie, that if needed, she would be glad to pay for summer school. So, Dad decided to stay. After the summer sessions ended, Dad hitchhiked from South Carolina back home to New Jersey for a short break. Dad told his mom, Alice Mae, about the weekend extension ministries he had the opportunity to participate in. She in turn told his dad, Edward, that they needed to help get him a car.

A car was found—an old '34 Pontiac. Dad's Great Uncle Vic bought it for $34. The car had a cloth hood. In the few short weeks left between summer school and the next school year and with a great deal of persistence, Vic and Dad cleaned up that car. They got new seats and bumpers and redid the engine. The car ended up selling for $300. With the money, Dad and Vic bought a 1938 Ford Coupe with a front bench seat.

That Ford Coupe proved to be a great fit for Dad's tenacious spirit. Back at school, Dad drove hundreds of miles most weekends to preach at small churches. One weekend, Dad drove all the way to Wisconsin.

Another time, because Dad's Ford Coupe sat up high enough, it allowed him to drive two miles up a creek to get to the country church where he was speaking. Dad's weekends off from traveling included Saturday Vesper rehearsals followed by two Sunday afternoon BJU Vesper performances.

Dad used the summers after his sophomore and junior years to travel with BJU ministry teams—playing his trombone, singing, and preaching. Even with all his extracurricular ministry, Dad was able to graduate with a double major in music and Bible in just three and a half years.

Dad's tenacity—perseverance, determination, and persistence—served him well all his years. Tenacity was the secret ingredient that God used not only for Dad's ministry preparation years, but also for all he accomplished for Jesus Christ the rest of his life.

7 DAD TAUGHT ME
HOW A HUSBAND SHOULD TREAT A WIFE

> *So ought men to love their wives as their own bodies. He that loveth his wife loveth himself. For no man ever yet hated his own flesh; but nourisheth and cherisheth it, even as the Lord the church.*
> —*Ephesians 5:28-29*

In Dad's freshman year, January 1949, Dad signed up for a voice class at BJU. This class is where he first saw Mom, Flora Jean Fox. He thought she looked like a doll and forever after they began dating, called her "My doll." Dad also loved Flora Jean's singing voice.

Because Mom was so popular and dressed so nicely, Dad thought, "She'll never be interested in me." He hadn't learned yet that she came from a humble upbringing and that she had even made all her own clothes.

Two years later, on Thursday of Bible Conference week in 1951, Mom and Dad's choir was walking up the steps of Rodeheaver Auditorium to go record for the BJU radio station. Dad asked Mom, "How about we sit together in the next Bible Conference service?" Mom said, "Ok." After that first service, they knew immediately they wanted to be together forever. Afterwards, Dad asked Mom to sit with him the next day, for Friday's morning service. She already had a date. Dad thought this meant, "Katie, bar the door."

Fortunately, a friend acted as a go-between telling Dad, "Listen. It's not that she doesn't want to go with you. She just didn't want to break her prior commitment." This same friend got them together for lunch that same Friday. Mom and Dad talked it through, and the rest is history. Three weeks later, Dad asked Mom to marry him. They were married within nine months, on January 3, 1952.

Mom and Dad's union was truly a match made in heaven. They loved to think that God had predetermined their marriage from the womb. They shared an interesting set of details. At some point they put their two stories together.

When Grandma Alice was four months pregnant with Dad, the doctors told her she was going to lose him. That's when Dad's parents passionately dedicated him to the Lord. Mom's story was identical: When Mom's mom was also four months pregnant, she was told the same thing, and she consequently dedicated her daughter to the Lord's service as well.

Dad treated Mom like a queen. My momma had a strong will. After Mom passed, Dad told me stories of how, behind the scenes, he had to be firm with her when needed. Dad remained loving and kind because that's who he was.

Mom took care of Dad too. Most don't know that Mom picked out Dad's clothes, laying them out for him every evening for the following day. On Saturday nights, Mom put out one tie to go with his Sunday suit for the morning service and another for the evening service.

"Husbands, love your wives" could be equated to a man treating and handling his wife like a fragile, valued vase. This is how I'll always remember Daddy treating Momma. Later in life, Mom often said, "Frank is the best man God ever created."

8 DAD TAUGHT ME
GOD WASTES NOTHING HE ALLOWS

> *Now no chastening for the present seemeth to be joyous, but grievous: nevertheless afterward it yieldeth the peaceable fruit of righteousness unto them which are exercised thereby.* —Hebrews 12:11

After Mom and Dad got married, they traveled with an evangelist doing the music. After several months, Dad discovered that the preacher was neo-orthodox. The evangelist's wife said she wasn't neo-orthodox, but liberal. The couple used Bible terminology but didn't believe in the full authority of Scripture— Shakespeare was the word of God as much as the Bible.

The traveling team was invited to the home of Sebastian S. Kresge, the man who started Kmart. By the questions posed by Mr. Kresge, it was obvious to Dad that he wanted to hear the gospel. Kresge asked, "How do you know that Jesus lived?" Dad said, "Because He lives in my heart." Overhearing this, the evangelist interjected, "You can't say that."

This experience was the moment that showed Dad the gospel of Jesus Christ meant different things to different people. Mary Lou Fillier, who also traveled with the evangelist as a soloist, suggested that Dad investigate going to the Eastman School of Music in Rochester, New York.

So, in 1953, Mom and Dad moved to Rochester. Dad went to school in the day, slept a few hours, then worked at Kodak during the night. For thirty-five cents an hour, he printed pictures in the evening and Mom inspected them in the day. Dad stayed one year in Rochester, working on his master's degree in music. During this stint, on January 23, 1954, I was born.

Mom and Dad knew they wanted to call me Shelly but were still looking for a "proper" name for me. One night as Dad was working developing prints, a newborn picture came across his desk. The baby girl's name was Sherrilyn.

Dad went home and told Mom he found the perfect name for me. From that point on, I was to become Sherrilyn Joy—with the nickname, Shelly. Dad wrote me a song while Mom was still in the hospital:

**Sherrilyn, my Sherrilyn,
I'm falling in love with you.
Can't you see, I want to be
The one who's holding you?
When you smile, life seems worthwhile.
It fills my heart with glee.
And Sherrilyn, I'm wonderin',
If you'll come home with me.**

Dad's experience traveling with the new-orthodox couple, caused him to carefully evaluate the biblical accuracy of gospel lyrics. Especially troubling were those that portrayed Christ as a rebel or others that painted Mary Magdeline as a harlot and Christ as one of her many men.

God has a purpose for everything we encounter and wastes nothing He allows.

9 DAD TAUGHT ME
THE MEANING OF TRUE LOYALTY

> *Then shall I know that . . . ye are true men.*
> *—Genesis 42:34*

In 1954, three months after I was born in Rochester, New York, Dad moved our family down to Pensacola, Florida. He accepted the call to be music and youth pastor under Pastor Dolphus Price at Brent Lane Baptist Church. Dad had only partially completed working on his master's degree at Eastman but felt God's leading to go.

Pastor Price wanted Dad to start a Christian School the fall of the same year. Dad did so and became the principal. He bought the books and the furniture, hired the teachers, and did everything else involved in taking on such a venture. During this time, Mom and Dad became close friends with

Beka and Arlin Horton. Dad went to them for advice on what textbooks to buy for the new school.

While at Pensacola, our family of three grew to four. My brother Randy was born at Baptist Hospital on February 27, 1957. At the church, Dad grew the choir of five to twenty and was able to start an orchestra. The youth group Dad led and taught expanded as well. Multiple men from this teen ministry later became pastors, Christian leaders, and Christian school teachers.

During this stint at Brent Baptist, a deacon in the church approached Dad. He complained about Pastor Price and said, "I think we need to let Pastor go." Dad responded, "If Dolphus Price goes, I go." Dad later told Pastor Price that he should know what one of his deacons had said. Pastor Price chuckled, "That deacon also told me the same about you. I said, 'If Frank goes, I go.'" What a display of true loyalty from both men.

In the late 1950s, when Mom and Dad were living in Pensacola, Dad was invited to go preach at First Baptist Church in Mary Esther, Florida. (Mary Esther is just ten minutes from Navarre where he lived the last five years of his life with my sister Gina.)

After the evening service, the church gave Mom and Dad a check for coming. They unfortunately had no cash to buy supper. There were, however, two silver dollars in the glove compartment of their Volkswagen.

Mom said, "Can we use the money in the glove compartment to get a hamburger?" Dad replied, "No. We need to save that money for an emergency." Mom pleaded, "But I'm hungry."

Dad did not give in, even though it was about a two-hour drive back to Pensacola.

Years later, when Mom and Dad were visiting New York City, someone broke into their Volkswagen and stole the two silver dollars. Mom jokingly told Dad, "See, I told you that you should have bought me a hamburger." Dad told me he learned that loyalty to a happy wife was certainly far better than two silver dollars.

For almost seventy years, I witnessed my dad being a loyal employee, a loyal husband, a loyal dad, a loyal coworker, and foremost—a loyal follower of Christ. Through thick and thin, Dad remained loyal to the Savior he served and to those with whom he served.

10 DAD TAUGHT ME TO
HAVE A SERVANT'S HEART

> *Not with eyeservice, as menpleasers; but as the servants of Christ, doing the will of God from the heart. —Ephesians 6:6*

To begin this chapter, I would like to turn back in time to Dad's growing up years in Montclair, New Jersey. At the bottom of the hill below the Garlock home, was a big black dog that would jump on Dad's bicycle handlebars to scare him. Also, at the bottom of the hill lived a lady who owned the house that Dad and his family lived in. The rent was thirty-five dollars a month.

Dad's mom, Alice Mae, felt sorry for their landlady because she didn't have much money. The rent they paid was her only income. In the winter, the woman couldn't get to her outhouse because of the snow, so she used cans inside the house instead. Dad's mom would have him go clean out all her cans to be a help. Consequently, no job since has ever been beneath him.

In 1954, as I mentioned in the last lesson, Dad became the music pastor in Pensacola, Florida. When he candidated, some of the congregation was concerned about a highfalutin Eastman School of Music graduate leading their humble choir. Still, Dad was voted in.

On his first Sunday, Dad noticed rust on the floor in the men's bathroom. Monday morning, without telling anyone, Dad went to the store and bought disinfectant and a scrub brush. The rust from the men's bathroom floor, as well as the women's, was soon gone. Word spread like wildfire. Dad was accepted, not for his musical knowledge, but rather his servant's heart.

Dad displayed this servant's heart to his family too. He would kneel by my bedside most evenings to ask me how my day had gone. He did the same for Randy and Gina.

At these nighttime chats, I would discuss both joys and problems I had faced that day. He would rejoice with me, console me, and give wise advice. Dad and I would often pray for the man that I would someday marry. Those times were priceless and drew my heart to his.

Now, to go forward in time—Mom got dementia in the last years of her life. She began to show concerning signs. Once, Mom forgot to turn the gas range off after leaving the kitchen. Another time, she wandered out the front door, and it took a while to find her.

Dad eventually moved himself and Mom—together—into Shepherd's Care Assisted Living in Greenville, South Carolina. Dad resolutely and simply explained to me, "Your mom followed me cheerfully all over the world. She, without complaining, stayed home and took care of you kids when I had to travel without her. Wherever she goes, I go."

While living at Shepherd's, Mom escaped from the building several times. Dad was told that for her safety, she needed to go into the memory care lockdown section of the facility. Dad refused for her to go without him, but insisted he would *not* go. So, my sister Gina and her husband David moved Mom and Dad down to Florida to live with them until Mom passed with Dad by her side.

As I cared for my husband Ron who also had dementia at the same time as my mom, my dad provided an example of how one should selflessly take care of a spouse. I learned true servanthood from Dad.

A servant is someone who does something for someone else even when that someone is unable to do anything in return.

11 DAD TAUGHT ME
TO GIVE IS BETTER THAN TO RECEIVE

> *It is more blessed to give than to receive.*
> *—Acts 20:35*

After three and a half years of ministering in Pensacola, Dad felt the need to return to Eastman and get more training. So, shortly after Randy was born, our small family packed up and moved back to Rochester, New York.

While there, Dad finished his master's degree and began working on his doctorate. A small Baptist church, Taylor Chapel, asked Dad to be their music pastor. Mom and Dad also became involved in doing the music for Youth for Christ meetings.

At Eastman, Professor Macose was Dad's music theory teacher. Dad was in his element in music theory. Macose, who authored music textbooks, used Dad as his assistant to help him grade theory papers. Macose told his class, you are the cream of the crop of musicians. Yet only one percent of you will be able to make music your full-time profession. Dad became part of that one percent.

In 1960, Dr. Gustafson from Bob Jones University gave Dad a call. Dr. Gus asked him to come down to Greenville, South Carolina and teach music theory and trombone. Dad explained to him that he lacked only sixteen hours to complete his doctorate work at Eastman. Dr. Gus was persistent, "We need you now." Dad felt this was God's leading him. He accepted. To Greenville, South Carolina we did go, and we have been serving in the same city ever since.

Wherever Mom and Dad served, they loved helping missionaries. Nothing gave them greater pleasure than spoiling them. In fact, after they got married, they prayed about being missionaries themselves and serving in Africa. They eventually were convinced that God wanted them to stay in the States and minister in music.

Over the years, Dad supported many missionaries, both personally and via the Southside Sunday School class he taught. During Mom and Dad's lifetime, they traveled to fifty different countries visiting missionaries. Some told them that this was their first visit from anyone in the States.

When missionaries would come into town, Mom and Dad often had them over for dinner. They also delighted in taking the missionaries shopping to buy new clothes instead of digging through pre-owned ones from mission barrels. Dad enjoyed collecting funds for talented Brazilian and Hispanic kids to go get musical training from Pensacola Christian College (PCC). Some are still serving at the school today. My parents were "giving people."

I was told a story recently by my first piano teacher, Mrs. Muriel Murr: The Murrs and my parents worked at BJU at the same time. Both couples were willing to serve there for a small salary. Once when Dad was at the mall, he ran into Muriel's husband, Dick. Dick was looking for a birthday present for his wife and was having trouble finding something he could afford.

Dad reached into his wallet and pulled out a twenty- or hundred-dollar bill—I can't remember which. Dick was then able to buy Muriel a beautiful dress. Mrs. Murr later told me she had kept that dress all this time. When I told Dad about Mrs. Murr's story, he said, "Muriel was so grateful. She brought our family a loaf of freshly baked bread every Sunday afternoon thereafter."

Dad gave everything—his time, his talent, his money, and his knowledge. Dad taught me that you live with your hands either outstretched or clutched closely to you. Things never matter as much as people.

To give is better than to receive.

12 DAD TAUGHT ME
MORE THAN JUST A MUSIC LESSON

> *And thou shalt teach them diligently unto thy children, and shalt talk of them when thou sittest in thine house, and when thou walkest by the way, and when thou liest down, and when thou risest up.*
> *—Deuteronomy 6:7*

Music and family were big parts of Dad's world. So naturally, he wanted his children to be musicians. Now at Bob Jones, our beloved family grew to five. In 1963, my sweet sister Gina Gay was born at the old BJU hospital, the present left wing of the Academy quadrangle. When Mom was pregnant with her, I prayed hard that the newborn baby would be a girl. Dad told me, "Shelly, the baby could be a boy." I said, "If it is, God can change it." And as it turned out, I got a sister. Now our family was complete.

As Randy, Gina, and I were growing up, Dad was determined we would learn *discipline* by practicing the piano. Dad had learned it by practicing the trombone. As a child, he would faithfully practice down in the basement of the family home. When he had trouble getting a certain passage of music, he would play it repeatedly until he mastered it. His siblings would call down to the basement and say, "Frank, play something else."

Once, Dad heard one of them say, "Frank will never amount to anything." He told me, "This comment didn't break me like you might think but rather made me determined to practice even harder." I believe this helped give Dad the discipline in life to accomplish all that he did.

When my siblings or I sat down to practice the piano, Dad often came in, sat down with us, and assisted. Because I loved the piano, I looked forward to these sessions. Dad would play the right hand as I would play the left hand. Then vice versa. If I made a mistake in the middle of the piece, I wanted to go back to the beginning and start all over. Dad would make me play the offending measure(s) over and over until I mastered it. Then and only then, could I go back and start the piece from the beginning.

Dad also made me practice my pieces with a metronome so I would learn how to stay in time with something other than myself. This was egregious to me at the time, but oh, how I now treasure the lesson of staying in sync with other musicians. Often, an hour or two of practice time would go by before I realized it.

Piano practice with Dad was more than just a music lesson. Dad taught me that perfection in performance rarely exists. We don't strive for perfection, but for excellence. Pursuing excellence in one aspect of life transfers to pursuing it in everything. The diligence it takes in the journey of excellence has helped in my schoolwork, music arranging, publishing, producing, writing, performing, as well as public speaking. Pursuing excellence develops strong character qualities within the one going after it.

Excellence was something that Dad was always diligently teaching the next generation. He even wanted to use his musical talent to help young children, ages three to five, develop strong character. All his grandchildren call him Pop-Pop. How will we ever forget *Pop-Pop's Teeny Tunes*—songs such as "Do you have to cut my toenails?" And we will always remember the lyrics that mimicked real car rides with little ones: "Are we there yet? O why does it have to take so long to get where we want to go? Are we there yet? We've sung every song we know to sing and some that we didn't know . . . "

One of Dad's children's songs that has become a favorite is "Do Right."

Do right till the stars fall.
Do right till the last call.
Do right when there's no one else to stand by you.
Do right when you're all alone.
Do right though it's never known.
Do right since you love the Lord.
Do right. Do right.

13 DAD TAUGHT ME
HARD WORK PAYS OFF

> *For thou shalt eat the labour of thine hands: happy
> shalt thou be, and it shall be well with thee. —
> Psalm 128:2*

In Dad's growing up years, he oversaw the ironing for the
entire Garlock family of twelve. He didn't let the time go to
waste but instead listened to preaching on the radio while he
worked. Through daily household chores and through living
his childhood in poverty, Dad learned the value of hard work.
Since then, no grass has ever grown under Dad's feet.

Dad always kept an unbelievably rigorous schedule. I remember
when I was in my teen years, Dad would teach all week, fly
out Friday night to speak on the dangers of rock music, fly
back Saturday night to teach his Sunday school class of five
hundred the next morning, and then conduct the morning
music service.

Additionally, one Sunday a month, Dad's BJU Vesper choir would sing two identical performances in the afternoon. Dad would then go back to church and lead the Men of Praise men's group, direct the Southside 150-member choir rehearsal, lead the congregation of 2000 in the Sunday evening worship, go home and grade his student's music theory papers, sleep a very little, and go right back to teaching Monday morning. "Hard work" was Dad's middle name.

In between all his obligations, Dad wrote music arrangements for the BJU faculty brass quintet, his traveling summer ministry brass quartets, and his Vesper choir. People started requesting the choral and brass pieces Dad arranged. So, Dad took his work ethic and started a sacred music publishing company in 1972. The company he began was called Musical Ministries (MM) and later was changed to Majesty Music.

With his new company, the first music conference Dad held was at Southside Baptist Church where he ministered. There were 150 music directors in attendance from all over the country. Fifty years later, Majesty Music Conferences are still in existence and Majesty continues to publish sacred music for adults and children alike. The ministry to date has been led by three generations—first the Garlocks, then the Hamiltons, and now the Morgans.

Dad often told me that one should take care of the depth of his ministry and God would take care of the breadth.

Contrary to what people may think, sacred music publishing is not a money-making pursuit. Dad told Ron and me, "If you want to start a sacred music company, dig an oil well first to support it." I believe God blessed both Dad and Ron, due to their working around the clock, managing and writing for their music publishing company, their extensive traveling ministries, and their church music pastor positions. Each arm of Majesty Music has been closely knit together with the same goal to support Conservative Christian Music—CCM at its finest.

I will be eternally grateful for Dad's founding of Musical Ministries in 1973. With it, he laid the foundation and platform for Ron and me to join in 1978. We came on board, literally, right after my husband Ron lost his left eye to cancer and became Patch the Pirate. The rest is history.

Dad, your hard work paid off.

14 DAD TAUGHT ME
MUSIC SHOULD BE ALIVE

> *Likewise reckon ye also yourselves to be dead indeed unto sin, but alive unto God through Jesus Christ our Lord.*
> *—Romans 6:11*

A past member of Southside Baptist Church told me recently, "I'll never forget singing 'Blessed Assurance' in the congregation while your dad led. I can still see how animated his face was."

If you were fortunate enough to be a member of Southside in the 1970s and 1980s, you would understand why some referred to Southside as "Singside." The church auditorium came alive when Dad led the congregation in song.

As Dad led, you dared not take your eyes off him, or you might end up singing a solo. He loved to slow down or speed up sections of the music to portray the meaning of the lyrics. His hands carefully painted exactly how he wanted the worshippers to sing: loud, soft, slow, fast, with ritardandos and accelerandos, with crescendos and decrescendos, and meditatively or joyfully. He could change any of these musical elements in an instant.

Dad loved making the 2000-member congregation into a choir. Some evenings Dad would divide all the church members into parts. The sopranos sat together, the altos, the tenors, and the basses. Each section would practice their parts individually. I especially loved when the congregation sang "The Holy City." Dad wrote parts for his Bob Jones trombone choir as an accompaniment and strung them across the balcony. The music put goose bumps on your goose bumps.

Just like our family memorized Scripture, Dad had the church congregation memorize a hymn of the month. I love thinking about how many of the church members can probably still sing those hymns in their hearts today. Memorizing hymns, like memorizing Scripture, is a wonderful way to meditate on biblical truth.

Dad often said, "Church music should be so alive that if you cut it with a knife, it would bleed." So much of church music today has become dead, and a rock beat has been added to liven up the congregational singing. Dad said, church music should be so alive that a rock beat would be unnecessary.

Mom and Dad produced a choral book series called "Choral Arrangements Everybody Can Sing." Churches across the world loved these arrangements because

they were filled with life and simple for the singer. However, because Mom's piano accompaniments leaned toward the difficult side, people jokingly called them "Choral Arrangements Everybody Can Sing and Nobody Can Play."

In the Majesty Music Easter and Christmas musicals, we have wanted the gospel to be shared. The gospel, means "good news." Nothing is more life-giving than the gospel. It is the announcement that Jesus brought salvation to mankind to save them from their sin through His life on earth, death on the cross, and resurrection from the dead. This gift is offered to all who accept Jesus Christ into their hearts and lives.

Music that includes the gospel should have life everlasting.

The Edward Garlock homestead

L to R: Ed, Eunice, Bob, and Frank Garlock

Dad at age 16

Frank and Flora Jean, Bible Conference 1952

Frank and Flora Jean on BJU campus

Dad in BJU traveling ministry team

*Mom and Dad in BJU traveling
ministry team*

Frank and Flora Jean wedding, January 3, 1953

L to R: Dad, Randy, Mom, and me

The Frank Garlocks and the Dwight Gustafsons, 1960

L to R: me, Dad, Mom, and Randy

Dad's trombone choir at BJU

Mom and Dad

brother Randy and sister Gina

L to R: The Youstras, Garlocks, and Murrs, BJU

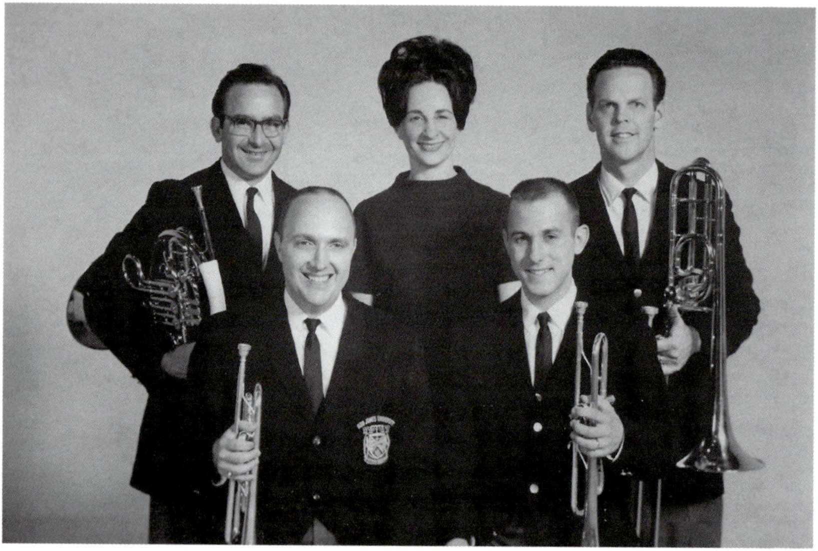

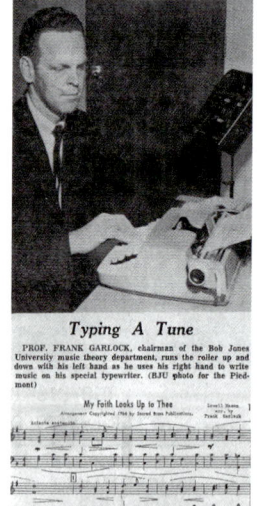

BJU traveling faculty quartet

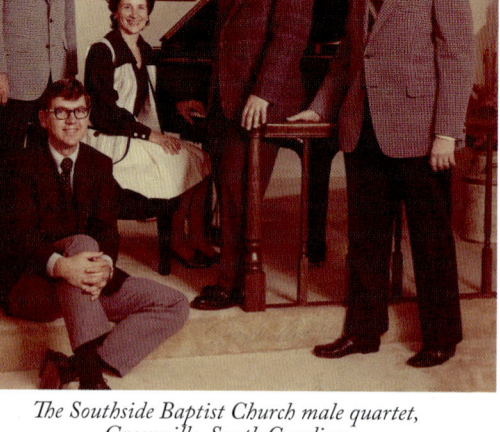

Typing A Tune

PROF. FRANK GARLOCK, chairman of the Bob Jones University music theory department, runs the roller up and down with his left hand as he uses his right hand to write music on his special typewriter. (BJU photo for the Piedmont)

My Faith Looks Up to Thee

THIS IS A SAMPLE of music written by Prof. Garlock on his special typewriter. The words across the top must be written in on another machine before the music is re-

First person in South Carolina to own a music typewriter

The Southside Baptist Church male quartet, Greenville, South Carolina

Dad's Cessna 172 airplane

L to R: Mom, Dad, Dr. Bob III, and Beneth Jones

Mom and Dad

Dad operating inside his plane

L to R: Pastor Walt Handford, wife Libby, Mom, and Dad

A vintage MusiCollege catalog cover photo

Mom and Dad sang lovely duets together

Mom and Dad at the Singapore Zoo while visiting missionaries

A glimpse into Dad's energy and enthusiasm while leading a congregation in song

L to R: Arlin Horton (from PCC), Dad, Mom, Beka Horton (from Abeka Books)

L to R: Mom, Dad, Ron Brooks, and Barbara Brooks

*Mom and Dad in their well-kept backyard—
one of my favorite pictures*

L to R: Mom, sister Gina, and Dad

*Dad teaching at Pensacola Christian
College in the master's music program he led*

Back row – L to R: Ron, me, Barbara Brooks, Ron Brooks, David Greene
Front row – L to R: Gina Greene, Judy Swaim, Mom, Joe Swaim

At son Jason's senior voice recital, BJU Chapel,
L to R: Adam Morgan, Megan Morgan, Ron,
me, Jason, Mom, Dad

Mom and Dad
Navarre Beach, Florida, 2019

My grandson, Hamilton Morgan with my dad

Dad and me in my kitchen

Dad and my son Jason

Dad and Ron at our home in Greenville, 2021

L to R: Dad, me, brother Randy, sister Gina

L to R: David Greene, Dad, me at Santa Rosa Sound

Dad's 92nd and last birthday party. I'm so glad I made his favorite—carrot cake

L to R: Dad, David, Ron, me, Gina, Jason at Dad's party in the Greene's dining room

David Price and Dad the day before he passed

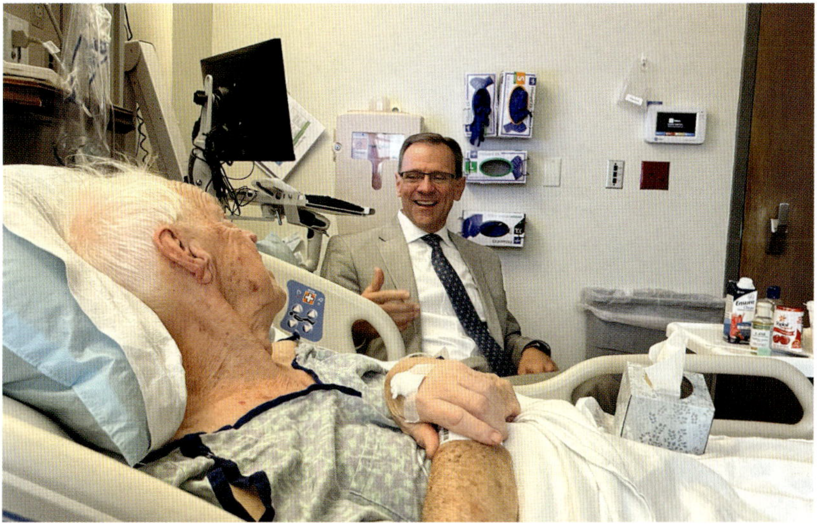

Dad in the hospital with Pastor Jeff Redlin

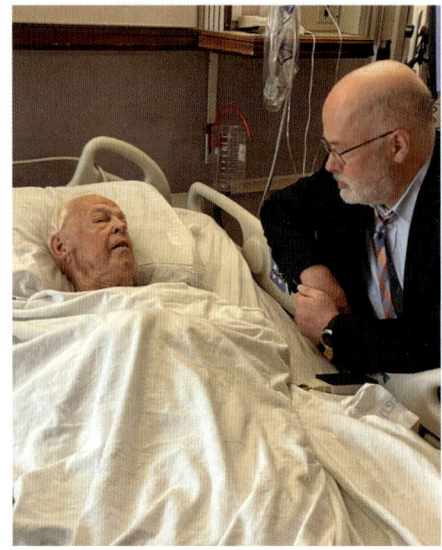

Evangelist Jim Schettler and Dad *Dad and his friend and assistant Tim Willingham*

L to R: My daughters Megs, me, Tara, Alyssa with Dad

15 DAD TAUGHT ME TO
BE FAITHFUL

> *Well done, thou good and faithful servant: thou hast been faithful over a few things, I will make thee ruler over many things: enter thou into the joy of thy lord. —Matthew 25:21*

In the 1960s there was a Rolling Stone concert in California where some concert goers were killed by members of the Hell's Angels motorcycle gang. Dad remembers commenting to Mom, "I wonder if the music had anything to do with the murders." Mom said, "The music is just a passing fad. I wouldn't spend any time looking into it." Wow, was she ever wrong. And as we now know, Dad didn't follow her advice.

In the 1960s, Dad spoke on rock music to the teens at Southside Baptist Church. Someone there heard the lecture and suggested to the leadership at BJU that Dad should give it to the students there. Dad next gave it to the Academy kids, then to the University. The lecture became a yearly event at the beginning of the school year.

Dad started being invited all over America to give this lecture. His first time giving it to a public high school in Greenville, South Carolina, over a thousand teenagers attended. The auditorium was so full that the overflow sat on the platform near where Dad was speaking. Sitting right next to him was a young man with no shirt on and who smelled of marijuana. Dad called his message "The Big Beat, A Rock Blast." Soon after, this very message at the public high school became available on an LP and in a book with the same title.

Rock music has become such a part of our culture, that many Christian young people today are conditioned to it. Dad never gave up but continued to write and speak about the dangers of its worldliness. The world's music has not gotten any better, but indeed worse.

Dad's faithfulness to speak out, though unpopular, is admirable. Recently, I heard a debate about "Aborting God?" The atheist on the debate said, "There is no afterlife. All that is important is our humanity now." He was wildly cheered as he went on to say, "Life is about drugs, sex, and rock 'n roll." In Dad's lectures years ago, this is exactly what he would say. He would then jokingly tell his skeptical audience, "You may not agree with me, but you've been wrong before."

Several years after Dad started speaking out on rock music, he eventually got his pilot's license and bought a private plane to help facilitate the multiple traveling opportunities.

Once, when landing at a small airport late at night, due to a rainstorm, Dad's plane hydroplaned off the runway into the nearby ocean. He had no idea how deep the water was where he landed, and the plane was slowly sinking.

Dad was able to get out of the plane and stand on one of the wings. He raised his hands and sang, "Great Is Thy Faithfulness." He fortunately was not far out from the shore and was rescued easily. His plane, not so much.

I believe that because of Dad's faithfulness to God, God was faithful to him.

16 DAD TAUGHT ME TO
BE DILIGENT

> *Therefore, as ye abound in every thing, in faith, and utterance, and knowledge, and in all diligence, and in your love to us, see that ye abound in this grace also. —2 Corinthians 8:7*

Dad diligently taught the Word of God to his family. Growing up, Randy, Gina, and I remember the times our family memorized Scripture passages together after dinner. We memorized entire chapters like 1 Corinthians 13, James 1, Hebrews 11, and Psalms 121. I loved these times but did not understand the full extent of what God was gifting us for our future lives.

Dad also had the vision to set up a "family appreciation night." Sometimes at dinner, one family member was chosen to be the recipient. After we ate, we went around the table and each of us said one thing about the family member that we appreciated.

Dad believed, "When you open your mouth to praise someone, you open your heart to them."

Dad was diligent in his ministry. Musical Ministries began with a staff of two—Dad and his secretary Bobbie Scrivner. Bobbie worked out of the garage of our home on Bob Jones campus. When Ron and I came on board in 1978, the ministry grew to six employees—Dad, Ron, Bobbie, Ron's sister Marty, Glenn Christianson, and me. We moved the ministry to the basement of a house a block away from the university campus. Ron and I lived on the first floor, and Marty lived in the loft on the second floor.

Because the MM staff increased, this office set-up did not last long. By 1980, Dad had bought an old building on Wade Hampton Boulevard, just a mile from BJU. This building was originally used for making mattress springs. My Uncle Bob refurbished the building into offices and a warehouse. I remember every morning, Dad going from desk to desk and praying for each individual staff member before they arrived and the workday started.

Dad was diligent in his teaching. Even though he already had a degree in music from BJU, when Dad arrived as a student at the Eastman School of Music, he was placed in music theory 101. When he went back to Bob Jones as a teacher, he vowed this would never happen to one of his students. In fact, when Dad arrived in 1960, Dr. Gustafson asked him to teach all the music theory faculty. As you can imagine, this endeared him to their hearts. As the music theory faculty grew in knowledge, the entire BJU music department became one of the best music programs in the country.

Wherever Dad went, I've already mentioned he had to start at square one. This was true at Eastman, Brent Baptist Church, Bob Jones University, the Southside Baptist Church choir, and his Southside Sunday School class. Dad also started at square one with rock music lectures, the music program at the Baptist University in Mexico, the master's program at Pensacola Christian College, and the Majesty Music publishing company.

Dad's diligence in serving God with his talents was rewarded with God's blessings on Dad's ministry efforts.

17 DAD TAUGHT ME
CONSISTENCY MATTERS

> *Therefore, by beloved brethren, be ye stedfast,
> unmoveable, always abounding in the work of the
> Lord, forasmuch as ye know that your labour is not
> in vain in the Lord.*
> *—1 Corinthians 15:58*

**Dad was extremely consistent, especially with
his grammar. Our family lovingly called him the
"grammar sheriff." When we brought Dad home
from the hospital two weeks before he passed,
Reagan asked him, "Pop-Pop, do you want to lay
down?" He just looked at her like he did not hear
her. So, Reagan repeated even louder, "Do you
want to lay down?" He simply raised his eyebrows.**

Then, Reagan realized her mistake. "Pop-Pop, do you want to lie down?" He responded, "In that case, yes!"

///////////

Someone finally reaching the ripe old age of ninety-two might think his circumstances warranted sitting back in an easy chair, sipping tea, and eating bonbons. Not Dad. He was not only diligent, but also consistent in that diligence. I tend to go ninety miles an hour but then crash. Whatever Dad set his mind to do, he consistently followed it through, never tiring.

Early one morning several years back, when I was visiting David and Gina's home in Florida, I walked up to the glass doors facing Santa Rosa Sound. I thought I saw a dolphin out in the water. I got so excited and stepped outside to get a closer look. I received the surprise of my life when I realized the dolphin was none other than Dad swimming back and forth, dock to dock. I became frightened that Dad's morning routine was too dangerous—that a shark might attack. Consequently, to ease my fears, rather than Dad quitting his routine, David put a swimming pool in their backyard for him to safely swim.

A typical day for Dad in his nineties was rising at 6 a.m., swimming in the pool, grabbing his own breakfast, taking out the trash, emptying the dishwasher, working on his computer writing a new book, practicing the piano from the hymnal, snacking on a few different salads for lunch, making a daily grocery run to Walmart and walking around the store for exercise, coming home and practicing his trombone, taking a short nap, reading, riding his bike around the neighborhood, eating supper with the family, washing the pots and pans, and then back to his computer to work on the podcasts he recorded with his right-hand man, Tim Willingham.

Dad invented the word consistent. Dad was consistent in physical exercise till the day he went into the hospital with cancer. Daid said,

"A body in motion, stays in motion."

He ran, rode his bike, swam, went roller blading, walked—whatever kept him active.

One of Dad's PCC friends, Steven Ainsworth, recently told his wife, Marty, that he thought it was time to stop playing his horn. Steven is in his mid-sixties. Marty told him, "You can stop playing your horn as soon as Dr. Garlock stops playing his."

Well, Steven, I hate to tell you, but I imagine Dad is still playing a trombone in heaven.

18 DAD TAUGHT ME
MORALITY EXISTS WITHIN THE ARTS

> *Proving what is acceptable unto the Lord.*
> *—Ephesians 5:10*

One lesson that Dad intentionally and passionately taught not only me, but thousands of others across the world, was that morality exists within the arts. Dad, as a musician, focused on teaching that there is morality in music, specifically rock. It seemed fitting that his teaching on this topic should be included in this book.

Dad believed, as well as Ron and me, that although the tools used in the creating of different arts are inanimate, the resulting piece of art is not. A canvas, paintbrush, and red paint cannot be considered moral objects. But when combined in the hands of an artist, a moral or immoral painting is achieved.

Humans are never neutral creatures. Therefore, any art or media created by a human will not be neutral as well.

A piece of paper, a pen, and letters of the alphabet cannot and will not be moral. However, when combined to create poems and stories, the results can be construed as moral or immoral.

Some Christian musicians argue that a piano or one of its keys cannot take on a moral quality. Therefore, the resulting music cannot be moral or immoral. Dad, Ron, and I assert that individual notes and rhythms, when combined to create a piece of music, can take on moral quality.

When debating whether music can be moral or amoral, the only people I have found that claim music is neutral are proponents of Christian rock. I say, "Interesting."

I end this lesson with the editor's note written by Mark Moring of *Christianity Today*, March 2011: "As often happens when discussing church music in the pages of *Christianity Today*, the articles display a bias for traditional music. This is unfortunate, because we at CT happen to also like contemporary worship music. We strove to find an article or conduct an interview that would give more space to exploring the gift of contemporary music, but came up empty. I'll be frank: When it comes to contemporary Christian music, I have yet to find authors who are able to probe its uniqueness with the same depth and insight as those who relish traditional music. What I usually find is articles that say, 'But people like it!'"

I must conclude that morality exists within the arts.

19 DAD TAUGHT ME
CIRCUMSTANCES NEED NOT DETERMINE DESTINY

> *But as for you, ye thought evil against me; but God meant it unto good. —Genesis 50:20*

Dad's first bike had only one pedal. He would ride it from their Verona home to downtown Park Avenue. People would laugh. Because Dad didn't let embarrassment of his one-pedaled bike deter him, he was eventually rewarded with a two-pedaled bike and then some.

Grandma Sadie Campbell started making fudge to sell so she could buy Dad's brother Ed a trombone. She made so much money that Dad was able to buy a trombone for Ed with some money to spare. The money left over bought Dad a bike that had both pedals.

Dad then received Ed's old trombone. Dad rode that bike from Verona to Caldwell Baptist Church each Sunday, trombone in tote, to play along with the congregational singing.

I asked Daddy, "Do you think this experience helped teach you to be strong when people were critical of your teaching on rock music?" He replied, "I guess it could have been."

Dad had two prayers when fighting against rock. First, he prayed God would keep him sweet in the battle. Second, he prayed that he, himself, would not be caught by the very thing he was fighting. Dad told me, "We don't judge people, we judge things." We study to know what is righteous and what is not.

Once, when a famous public speaker was asked to preach at a large convention in Atlanta, Georgia, the speaker had to cancel at the last minute. This speaker was going to be accompanied by a well-known Christian rock group. Dad was immediately called to step in and, no joke, speak about rock music.

At the beginning of the meeting, when it was announced that Dad was going to speak on the evils of rock, half of the 2,000 people gathered got up and walked out. As Dad began speaking, people continued to exit until only about 500 were left. Dad, as he always did, concluded with the gospel. About 60 people came forward that night to get saved.

One of Dad's favorite people was Dr. Ben Carson. He admired him because he saw some similarities in their life stories. Dr. Carson grew up in a poor, broken home. He did not do well at school and was called "Dummy" by his classmates.

Ben's mother determined that Ben and his brother would do better. She insisted they go to the library once a week, check out two books, then write a paper on what they had read. She checked the reports, although Ben and his brother had no idea that she was unable to read them. After arriving home from school, the television was not to go on until both brothers had read from their books. Interestingly, their favorite programs became brain-teaser game shows.

Very soon, Ben became the smartest boy in the class instead of the dumbest. Much later, after becoming a brain surgeon, Dr. Carson was able to perform the first successful separation of Siamese twins, and he eventually became one of the most well-known brain surgeons in the world.

Dr. Ben Carson teaches the truth not to be victims, but victors.

**A victim walks through sand and sees only dirt.
A victor walks through sand and sees the ingredients for building a sandcastle.**

Similarly, Dad's circumstances as a youngster could have made him bitter, but he became better, proving your circumstances do not have to determine your destiny.

20 DAD TAUGHT ME TO
HAVE A SONG IN MY HEART

And he hath put a new song in my mouth, even praise unto our God. —Psalm 40:3

Dad always had a song in his heart, and it was obvious to everyone. Charlie Arbetell, my husband Ron's Florida hospice chaplain during his bout with dementia, became friends with Dad as he made visits to see Ron. The two grew to know each other well. Dad and Charlie had shared memories, a mutual love for Jesus, and music. Charlie called me recently and said, "I woke up this morning thinking of your dad. Two words came to mind—'joy unspeakable.'"

Some years ago, Dr. Tom Kendall told Dad after one of his doctor visits, "You always come in here with a smile on your face. Many patients, being sick, are negative and complain about this and that. You, however, are always positive and lift my spirits."

Indeed, Dad's joy flowed from his being. There seemed to be a continual song in his heart. Being a man of God gave him the joy of the Lord. Throughout the Bible, men of God talk about Him being their song.

Moses said it when leading the Israelites out of Egypt:

> *"The Lord is my strength and song, and he is become my salvation: he is my God, and I will prepare him an habitation; my father's God, and I will exalt him."*
> *—Exodus 15:2*

David said it when nations compassed about to try to destroy him:

> *"The Lord is my strength and song, and is become my salvation."—Psalm 118:14*

Isaiah the prophet, whose name means salvation, wrote about it:

> *"Behold, God is my salvation; I will trust, and not be afraid: for the Lord Jehovah is my strength and my song; he also is become my salvation."—Isaiah 12:2*

When Dad came to BJU to teach in 1960, he bought the trombone he has had ever since—a Conn 88-H.

Interestingly, Dad's trombone teacher at Eastman, Emory Remmington, has had a trombone student in every famous orchestra in the United States. Dr. Remmington designed the mouthpiece for the Conn 88-H trombone.

Dad was very proud of that trombone. In fact, the song in his heart came out through his trombone. He could make that trombone sing. In addition, Dad always taught his students to "sing into the instrument." Playing your trombone like you are singing makes the tone beautiful. Dad said, "Anybody who knows can tell the difference."

God created music to be a gift to mankind. I often wonder what heaven's music will be like. My guess—like food, it will have similarities but be more delicious. Like a flower, it will have similarities but be more beautiful. Like animals, they will have similarities but be more loveable. Our friend, Jim Schettler, mentioned the gold streets in heaven might perhaps be translucent because of having no impurities. Everything in heaven will be more wonderful.

Heaven's music will be the most glorious and joyful music ever. David, the Psalmist, said, "God hath put a new song in my mouth." New doesn't necessarily mean "new different," but a "new quality"—a quality unimaginable. Dad carried a "song" within his heart.

To me, Dad's life was a song, and that song was Jesus.

21 DAD TAUGHT ME TO
BUY HIGH, SELL LOW

You have heard: "Buy low, sell high." Randy and I have often joked about Dad comically reversing this good advice. Gina doesn't take part in our jesting. But it was true. So true that Dad even joked about it himself. Dad knew he wasn't perfect and was able to laugh at his weaknesses—another lesson in and of itself.

One incident might give you a little insight. Dad was invited to go speak at a church in Wilmington, North Carolina. After accepting the engagement, Mom realized that Myrtle Beach was on the way. Dad had the brilliant idea to take the used camper he had recently purchased and take Mom along with Ron and Barbara Brooks for a fun getaway. Ron and Barbara were so close to our family that we called them Uncle Ron and Aunt Barbara.

When Dad bought the camper, he was assured by the salesman that if it didn't behave properly, he could bring it back for a full refund. The evening before the getaway with the Brooks, Dad tried out the generator. However, it would not turn on. He drove the camper to a shop, only to find out the offending part could not be fixed. A new one would need to be ordered. No time for that. They could hook up to electrical outlets on their stops.

The night before the camper excursion, the camper was packed and resting peacefully in Dad's driveway. The slide out worked and was fully extended. Yes, it indeed was going to be a fun little vacation for the Brooks and the Garlocks.

Following a good night's sleep, the morning arrived for their departure. Try as he might, Dad could not get the slide *out* to slide *in*. After about thirty minutes of tinkering around with it, it finally behaved and retracted. Dad then went and released the black valve at the bottom of the camper for the trip. Horrible substances hit him in full force. No problem. Dad went into the house, cleaned up, and changed. It was now time to get the tow dolly for the jeep.

Dad successfully backed out of the driveway and headed to David and Gina's house just down the street to get their tow dolly. Multiple cars were parked in the driveway behind the needed dolly. After Dad got the keys and moved all the cars, he was finally able to get the dolly to the back of the camper and attached. All the cars were returned to the driveway. Time for Dad to go back to his house, the camper and dolly in tow, to get the jeep.

Once the jeep and Mom were loaded up, they headed over to get Uncle Ron and Aunt Barbara. Uncle Ron had warned Dad that it might be hard to turn the camper around because of the cul-de-sac at the end of their street. "No problem," was Dad's response. Well, when Dad arrived at the Brooks' home, a car was parked in the cul-de-sac. Oops. In trying to maneuver the camper around the parked car, the camper came slightly off its bed. Uncle Ron and Aunt Barbara stared in disbelief and horror.

Uncle Ron went into his garage and got a wrench. First, the jeep had to come off the dolly. Next, the dolly had to come off the camper bed. Finally, with some proper wrench turns, the camper rested back properly in place. Dad was able to reattach the dolly to the camper and get the jeep back on the dolly. Now, the entire rig could be turned around.

Time to go. The trip fortunately went successfully from the Brooks' home to the beach. Dad pulled the camper into a campground rented space and took the jeep off the dolly. The trouble now was that the jeep wouldn't start, and worse, it had been unloaded in the middle of the park driveway.

Uncle Ron was able to find another car owner who was willing to help them jumpstart the jeep. In the meantime, Dad tried to hook up the sewage and electrical for the camper. The trouble was, he hadn't pulled the camper in far enough. Well, that was soon remedied, so they thought. However, the hook up sewage nozzle didn't have the correct attachment. Dad, in his attempt to get it hooked up, sprayed sewage on the camper parked next to theirs. Oops.

Dad and Uncle Ron went to the park attendant to ask where they could go to get the needed attachment. Simple—Walmart sold it. The jeep was now running, but Dad had shut the jeep door and it automatically locked. They knew where to go but couldn't get in the vehicle to take them there. They had to call AAA to come unlock the jeep. The crew of four loaded up in the now running jeep and took off, only to find out upon arrival that Walmart didn't have the needed part.

An EMT at the gas station near where the camper was parked overheard Uncle Ron and Dad talking about their needed attachment. He directed them to another store that his friend owned, just thirty minutes away. The issue was that it closed in thirty minutes. The man called his owner friend, who said he'd wait for them to arrive. In fact, the EMT was headed in the same direction and said he'd lead them there. They took off.

Whew! Bullet dodged. The crew made it in time to get the needed part. By this time, all were starving. The EMT gave them the name of the only restaurant within driving distance. Off they went to The Front Porch restaurant. After they ate, the weary travelers headed back to the camper. Upon arrival, all were too exhausted to go see the beach. Besides, it was dark. They put the needed attachment on the sewage line and went down for the night.

The next morning, upon rising, they had just enough time to get the dolly and jeep hooked back on the camper, undo the electrical and plumbing hookups, and leave. Very sadly, the traveling group never got to see the beach. Oh, well. They would have fun on the rest of the trip to get Dad to his speaking engagement.

When they pulled up to the church, they discovered their water hose wasn't long enough to reach the church's water source. Oh, well, no problem. There was a bathroom in the church they could all use only about one hundred yards away from the camper.

The meeting went well. Afterwards, as they were driving back home, they heard a clunk. The jeep had come loose from the dolly and was traveling down the road by itself. Panic! Fortunately, it took a sharp turn to the right and landed on the side of the highway. Dad pulled the camper over and backed up to the runaway jeep. He and Uncle Ron crawled underneath the jeep and tried to reattach the chain. A policeman spotted them and knowing what to do, came to the rescue. Back home they finally did go.

Obviously, Dad took the camper back to where he bought it to get his refund. Nope! The salesman didn't remember ever saying anything of the sort. Dad did get some of his money back and resolved never to buy another camper again!

"Buy high, sell low" in full action.

22 DAD TAUGHT ME TO
REDEEM THE TIME

Redeeming the time, because the days are evil.
—Ephesians 5:16

In a previous lesson about Dad teaching me to have a servant's heart, I told the story of the Garlock's landlady for whom Dad helped clean out her buckets. This lady lived in one direction from Dad's house as he grew up in Montclair, New Jersey. Going in the other direction from Dad's house lived Mrs. Brown, a very nice lady. Dad's mom, Alice, would take a hambone and beans, cook them all day, and send them with Dad to give to Mrs. Brown.

Dad would go out to Mrs. Brown's garden and pick vegetables for her. Mrs. Brown had two sons who owned a moving company. They were unfortunately drunkards. Dad remembers

Mrs. Brown having a crack between where one of her walls and the ceiling met. One day, a mouse peeked its head out of that crack. Mrs. Brown's cat got that mouse in one leap.

In the dead of winter, Dad's oldest sister Eunice went to check on Mrs. Brown. When she arrived, the front door was partially ajar. Mrs. Brown's sons had left a window in her room open. She sadly had frozen to death. This incident gave Dad a life-long urgency to redeem the time.

Dad lived his life using time wisely. Before Dad died, he asked me, "How old are you? You are only sixty-eight, right? You have lots of time left to write." I'll never forget this comment. Was Dad encouraging me to redeem my time by writing?

In 2010, Dad was invited by our friend Sara Bennett to go to Haiti and teach music principles at the Hosannah Baptist Church in Jacmel. The first evening Dad was to speak, the music portion and a ladies skit took up most of the service time.

Dad decided to simply give the gospel that night. Many came forward to accept Christ into their hearts. The next day at 5:30 p.m., the destructive Haitian earthquake took place. Port-au-Prince and Jacmel were the two places hit hardest with its devastating effects. Dad's giving the gospel the previous evening was a God-thing.

Our family spent the week after the earthquake wondering if Sarah and Dad had made it out of the earthquake alive. Most communication went down. We finally reached the director of a nearby orphanage. She went out in her truck, drove down streets of neighborhoods to look for any sign of them. When she came upon Sarah's street, Dad was out for a walk. She spotted his white head from the pictures we had sent. Another God-thing.

Very unfortunately, many Haitians lost their lives that fateful day in January 2010. Sarah and her family had spent their lives telling them how to know Christ as their Savior.

Often the Haitians were procrastinators and would say, "Tomorrow." Heard all over Haiti directly following the earthquake were cries, "Lord Jesus, save me."

Yes, the best way to redeem the time is by reaching the world for Christ, because none of us knows how much time we will have.

23 DAD TAUGHT ME TO
"JUST SHOW UP"

> *"Be ready always to give an answer to every man that asketh you a reason of the hope that is in you."*
> —1 Peter 3:15

To just show up was on continuous play in Dad's life.

My baby sister, Gina Gay Garlock Greene, always said that she wanted to take care of Mom and Dad when they were old. This is exactly what she did for their last five years—Mom, until she died of dementia in 2019 and Dad, until prostate cancer took him in 2023. Gina learned the lesson well to just show up from Dad. And boy did he get to reap what he sowed with her.

Gina not only helped take care of Mom and Dad, but in 2022 she also willingly invited Ron, Alyssa, and me to move down to Florida and live with them. She offered this so that she could help me take care of Ron in his last stages of dementia. What sister would do that and furthermore, what brother-in-law would get on board? I still tell David often, "You are a good egg." He always responds with, "A little scrambled, and possibly a little cracked." So, in July 2022, Ron and I moved down to Navarre.

For years, Gina, Randy, and I watched Dad show up for so many people (many of whom I've already told you about). We also watched him show up for lonely difficult speaking engagements. I truly thought he enjoyed many of these things.

I thought that Dad, who had been a public speaker much of his life, was pumped to speak to crowds. Exactly a week before Dad got severely sick due to cancer, I was to go speak at a ladies' conference. In a moment of transparency, I shared with Dad some of my personal struggles.

I told him, "I dislike public speaking, so why do I accept? I have ANTs (automatic negative thoughts)—not when I accept, but as the time gets closer. I start remembering how much time it takes to prepare and how nervous I get." Surprisingly, Dad responded with, "I don't like public speaking either. I would get to the auditoriums, surrounded by hundreds of teenagers, and think to myself, 'What am I doing here?' But as soon as I got up to speak, away I went and was fine."

I was shocked. But his admission helped give me strength to bravely accomplish my upcoming speaking engagement.

Often, I feel like Moses, "O my Lord, I am not eloquent" (Exodus 4:10). God tells Moses in verse 12, "Now therefore go, and I will be with thy mouth, and teach thee what thou shalt say." I just need to be a willing instrument. When God gives me an opportunity to proclaim His goodness, all that's required of me is to "just show up!"

Dad also taught me, "If you speak to hurting people, you'll always have an audience."

Dad also authored his autobiography entitled, *I Being in the Way, the Lord Led Me*. He made these words from Scripture the theme of his life. As God had so clearly led Abraham's servant to find a wife for Isaac, God led Dad by his willingness to "be in the way" and to "just show up."

This lesson in particular has been a help to me in my daily spiritual walk. So often, I find myself not wanting to do something out of fear or selfishness.

Thank you, Dad, for paving the way I should go.

24 DAD TAUGHT ME TO
ALWAYS FORGIVE

> *And be ye kind one to another, tenderhearted,*
> *forgiving one another, even as God for Christ's sake*
> *hath forgiven you. —Ephesians 4:32*

In 2022-2023, Ron, Alyssa, and I were living with David
and Gina Greene due to Ron's dementia. One day, David
mentioned to me that I should talk to Dad about his driving.
Or maybe it could be Gina and I together, as his daughters.
Dad had always driven fast with quick driving responses.
He learned to drive in New York City traffic—if that tells you
anything about his driving.

Well, in his later years, his responses had slowed down, but
he wasn't aware of it. He often scared us all, including Tom
whom he picked up to come work at the Florida house. One
instance in particular, Tom saw his life flash before his eyes

as Dad pulled out onto busy I-98, right in front of a fast-approaching car.

I finally decided it was time to sit down with Dad and called Gina to come in as backup. "Dad, we love you. But you must slow down." I shared our concern and then relayed two instances where he had scared Tom with his driving.

Dad's response was good, as it always was: "I love you, too, and appreciate all your advice."

Now fast forward to several days later.

Gina yelled down to Dad from her upstairs bedroom, "Dad, can you go pick up Tom?"

Dad: "No."

Gina: "Dad, what?"

Dad: "Carrie is coming to pick me up soon to go to breakfast, and I'm mad at Tom."

Shelly: "Dad, don't be mad at Tom. It is all of us who are afraid of your driving."

Dad: "Ok, I'll go get him. But I don't want to."

Dad headed outside to the car. A few minutes later, he came back in. "There are two accidents out on I-98, and the traffic is at a standstill. I'll go a little later when it's cleared up."

Shelly: "Dad, please don't be mad at Tom. We're just concerned for you."

Dad: "I'm not mad."

Shelly: "But you said that you were."

Dad said: "I just got over it."

This is the only instance Gina or I ever remember Dad refusing to do something because he was upset at someone. And even then, it didn't last long.

I can also tell you many instances where Dad had reason to be angry about how he was treated or what someone said about him. He instead chose to forgive.

I learned from Dad,

"Bitterness is like drinking poison and hoping the other person will die."

Forgiveness is the only option.

25 DAD TAUGHT ME
PEOPLE ARE THE ONLY THING WE TAKE TO HEAVEN WITH US

> *And I will very gladly spend and be spent for you.*
> *—2 Corinthians 12:15*

Dad moved Mom down to Florida in 2017 due to her dementia. Gina helped Dad with her care, and Monica became her nurse. Although Mom passed in 2020, Monica stayed on to help Dad with his needs and meds. Monica loved Mom and Dad and vice versa. While she took care of Mom, Dad taught her many things about the Bible. She loved him so much that she asked him to perform her wedding ceremony in 2021.

In 2023, Gina had texted Monica about Dad's cancer prognosis, but unfortunately Monica had read it wrong. She misread it to say that Dad was getting better. When she arrived to visit

Dad after he returned home from the hospital, she was happy. Shortly after her cheerful greeting, Dad told her he only had a few weeks to live. She left in tears.

Monica was one of the many blessings God gave to Mom and Dad the last years of their lives. Monica is one of the many people Dad will have taken to heaven with him.

Since finding out how short Dad's time was to remain on earth, hundreds of people—a large percentage of them being missionaries, pastors, and music ministers—told us of the great influence Dad had on their lives. Many said he was their mentor. We knew Dad's spiritual involvement with people was large but had no idea how large.

People from all over the world started contacting us with their sympathies: Sheri Chavers (Nikki Chavers' wife), Evangelist Ben Everson and (his dad) Dana Everson, Pastor Jerry Mathias, Evangelist Jim Schettler, Pastor Paul Chappell, Mike Zachary, Pastor Jim Scudder, Dr. Bob Jones III, Mike Herbster, Carl Herbster, Larry Brubaker, numerous missionaries, and more.

When I think of Dad as a mentor, I think of Ron's and my son Jason. When Jason moved to Pensacola three years ago to go to PCC, Dad was still living at David and Gina's, not far from the campus.

Dad was able to spend hours with Jason. They weekly played their trombones in the school band together. Many times, they would grab supper at the school cafeteria. David Greene and Dad drove over to Pensacola for most Sunday morning services and then took Jason to lunch. Dad encouraged Jason in his studies.

When Jason became the intern music leader at Northstone Baptist Church, Dad went and played trombone duets with him. He instructed him how to play his trombone along with the congregational singing. After Dad passed, Jason grieved severely over the loss. Thank you, Dad, for helping my son and stepping in to be there for him when his dad couldn't.

Dad has been loved wherever he has gone. In Dad's later years, he continued investing in people's lives. As I've said, he never met a stranger. Whoever met Dad would hear some of his life stories or a summation of what he had learned from the latest book he was reading. In fact, one of Dad's caregivers once gushed to Gina, "I could listen to your dad all day." Gina responded, "Don't worry, you will." Dad had so much to share. His mind and his love never quit.

Dad also said,

"When you invest in people, you invest in eternity."

Dad knew the owner's names at the bakery, the Publix deli, the restaurants, and the gift shops. He took an interest in everyone he met and put many of them on the prayer list he kept on his phone. In fact, when I told the owners of the Navarre Bakery and the Coral Door gift shop of Dad's passing, they cried. When you invest your life in people, the returns are great.

Dad you were right, "people are the only thing we will take to heaven with us."

26 DAD TAUGHT ME
HUMOR HELPS

> *A merry heart doeth good like a medicine.*
> *—Proverbs 17:22a*

My dad not only *had* character, but *was* a character. He loved telling jokes and making people laugh. Even at Dad's funeral, someone came through the visitation line who had traveled with Dad on a BJU summer ministry team. He said, "Your dad could fill the monotony of traveling with joke upon joke."

If I got a fancy for ice cream before going to bed, and there wasn't any in the house, Dad would run to the store and get it. Cookies and ice cream became Dad's and my nightly ritual. After Ron and I were married, I wanted some ice cream before going to bed. I had been watching my weight, so Ron thought I shouldn't

indulge. I, however, eventually persuaded him to agree to my having one small bowl. I next reached for a cookie to go with my ice cream. In fun, Ron tried to grab it. I told him, "But Daddy and I always have cookies with our ice cream." This statement morphed into a family joke.

Over the last five years, I started a document on my computer called "Dad's Quips." I cannot write a book about my daddy without including at least some of his most often recited jokes. So, hang on—here goes!

I'm strong, but odor isn't everything.

I feel great, like the bottom of a stove.

I wanted to be discovered, but I got found out instead.

I have a photographic memory—it just hasn't been developed yet.

My memory is like Swiss cheese—it has holes in it. (When Dad said this once to Megan, she replied, "Aged to perfection.")

My favorite musical modulation is by cymbal crash.

Do you walk to school or carry your lunch?

Why does a plane have a propeller? To keep the pilot cool. Turn it off and watch him sweat.

My family was so poor, we ate apples for breakfast, drank hot water for lunch, and let them swell for supper.

Growing up, I was too poor to pay attention.

Please put on my tombstone, "I told you I was sick."

We're just going in circles, and we're not even big wheels.

Of all the things that I've lost, the thing I miss most is my mind.

It isn't the cough that carries you off; it's the coffin they carry you off in.

I may be dumb, but I'm not stupid.

A teacher asked a student to form a sentence using the words defeat, deduct, defense, and detail. The student said, "Defeat of deduct went over defense before detail."

Friend 1: The greatest invention in the world is the thermos jug.
Friend 2: Why's that?
Friend 1: In the summer it keeps drinks cold; in the winter it keeps drink hot.
Friend 2: What's so great about that?
Friend 1: How "do" it know?

Sonny the weatherman said: "I hope you enjoyed shoveling up the seven inches of partly cloudy I predicted last night."

Sonny the weatherman said: "I always wanted to be a weatherman, because it's the only place you can be wrong 50% of the time, and still keep your job."

A man went to a hotel and asked the porter what his average tip was. The porter responded, "Fifty dollars." The man gave him a fifty-dollar bill and said, "That's a little high for a tip, isn't it?" The porter said, "Yes. You're the first one that has come up to the average."

Some golfers were playing golf by a road. A funeral procession went by. One player stopped, took off his hat, and put his hand over his heart. The other players were surprised and questioned him about his actions. He responded, "That's my wife. She was a good woman."

One golfer sliced the ball and it hit a car in its windshield that was traveling down a road. This resulted in the car crashing into another car. The offending golfer said, "Oh, no—what am I going to do?" His buddy said, "When you hold the club, just move your hand a little bit to the left. That will solve your problem."

Two guys were playing golf. One of the golfer's friends had a stroke on the first hole and died. Somebody asked him, "So, what did you do?" He said, "Thereafter, it was 'hit the ball and drag Harry.' 'Hit the ball and drag Harry.'"

Two guys were standing on a bridge. One had a little box containing something he was trying to sell.
Friend 1: "What's in the box?"
Friend 2: "Pills of knowledge."
Friend 1: "What are they for?"
Friend 2: "They make you smarter."
Friend 1: "How much do they cost?"
Friend 2: "They're three for a dollar."
Friend 1: "If they really make you smarter, I'll take three."
Putting them in his mouth, he said, "These pills taste like manure."
Friend 2: "See. You're getting smarter already."

In Dad's small town of Verona, New Jersey, they had policemen called "pinchers." Parking spaces were so limited, if you didn't park at an angle within the lines, you got "pinched" or arrested. The pinchers walked up and down the two blocks of the downtown area to make sure all cars were parked according to specifications. Dad would joke, "A cracked chair is like a pincher. If you don't park right, you get pinched."

When Dad led choirs he told them, "No scooping when you sing. Let's save scooping for the ice cream parlor."

When someone entered our house, Dad would say, "Look what the cat dragged in."

When Dad opened the door for ladies to pass through and they said, "Thank you," Dad would respond, "I'd do the same thing for a friend."

Sometimes, when Dad complimented someone about something they had done, he would say, "You have over benefractured yourself."

When you kill a roach, a thousand come to its funeral.

A lady came up to a worker in the grocery store and said, "I'd like to buy just a half a head of lettuce." The worker went to his manager and said, "There's a crazy lady in the store who only wants to buy a half a head of lettuce." As he turned around, he saw the lady standing there. So, he said, "And this nice lady wants to buy the other half."

When I would call Dad late at night, I would say, "I hope I didn't awake you." Dad would reply, "No. I had to get up and answer the phone anyway."

Everything hurts, and what doesn't hurt, doesn't work.

It's hard to make a comeback when you haven't been anywhere.

I started out with nothing, and still have most of it left.

I believe five out of four people have trouble with fractions.

If you knows me, keep yo' mouth shut.

I'm so absent minded, I kiss the door and slam my wife goodbye.

Grape-Nuts®—where there are no grapes, and you can't find any nuts either.

I'm not as old as I look—I've just been sick a lot.

We're off—like a herd of turtles.

I don't know where Dad got this one, but instead of saying, "What a coincidence" he would say, "What a co-EEN-kee-dink!"

When Dad was asked if he wanted something offered him at a dinner, Dad would say, "Yes, I want everything that's coming to me." Once, Mom comically responded to Dad's common quip with, "One of these days, you're going to get it."

Once, when Mom and Dad were guests at someone's house for breakfast, the hostess asked them how they liked their eggs. Mom answered for them both, "We like our eggs sunny side up with pepper." Dad responded, "I don't like pepper on my eggs." Mom said, "I always put pepper on your eggs." Dad said, "I know."

Mom kept us laughing too: A special speaker came to Southside Baptist Church. After his message at the invitation, he said, "All those who want to be the leader of their home, please stand up." Mom, who was seated at the piano, only heard part of the question. She thought the preacher said, "All those who want their husband to be the leader of their home, stand up." Mom promptly stood up. When she saw Dad was standing, she motioned for him to sit down.

27 DAD TAUGHT ME TO
USE OUR MINISTRY TO BUILD PEOPLE

> *"For though I should boast somewhat more of our authority, which the Lord hath given us for edification, and not for your destruction, I should not be ashamed." —2 Corinthians 10:8*

Dad often said, "We don't use people to build our ministry, but our ministry to build people." When you are one of the heads of a ministry, building the people who work with you is critical to building your ministry.

When you are a person who is driven to get things done, you can sometimes run over the very people who are helping you get it done. Building up people is not a box that you check off a list. In fact, it is difficult to measure progress or success. You may not know for a long time if your efforts yield any fruit.

You may not ever know. But you still strive towards this goal. Building up people in your ministry is a mindset which only happens with intentionality. And believe me, it can be easier said than done.

If anyone understands this, I do. And I regret, I can be one of the worst offenders—not on purpose of course, but because time is so limited. I have dashed in and out of the office when music needed to be printed or filed, letters answered, or emails sent. I have often rushed back home to take care of the children and the home, then write more music. In the later years, I would rush back home to take care of Ron.

Fortunately, Majesty's traditions keep us close knit. Throughout the year we celebrate birthday parties, have special picnics together, and—as the climax to our year—come together for a staff Christmas party, complete with a hilarious white elephant gift exchange.

Dad was so good at building up the people of our Majesty Music family. He was of the belief that all MM staff should go to our church, Southside Baptist. His thought was that we would all be hearing the same preaching, and then we could talk about the sermons and what we were learning. As a result, we could grow together spiritually.

Many Majesty employees were in Dad's Sunday School class as well. Dad visited their homes, counseled them spiritually, and knew their prayer requests.

As I've already mentioned, when Dad was in town, he would

come to the office early and pray at each employee's desk for that person's needs. He could pray for those needs, because he knew them. That kind of knowledge takes time and intentionality. Dad would say,

"People don't care how much you know, until they know how much you care."

The employees that worked for Dad knew how much he cared. One of our now retired employees, Selita Hoffman, once went to a conference where the question was asked, "How many of you would work for your company, even if you didn't get paid?" Selita, a longtime, dedicated MM employee at the time, raised her hand. The facilitator at the conference repeated the question and then added, "I don't think you understood the question." Selita responded with, "Yes, I understand," and kept her hand up.

Also, building the people who are the beneficiaries of your ministry is critical to having a successful ministry. When you find out what people's needs are and then meet those needs, you will always have a ministry.

Each generation of the Majesty Music leadership is a little different, just as talents and personalities are different. Ron and Adam, following in Dad's footsteps yet gifted in their own way, have always kept this main goal the same: "Don't use people to build your ministry but use your ministry to build people."

28 DAD TAUGHT ME TO
HAVE A STRONG FINISH: JOURNALING DAD'S LAST DAYS

> *I have fought a good fight, I have finished my course, I have kept the faith.* —2 Timothy 4:7

Dad's life can be seen as a beautiful music composition, a ninety-two-page cantata. As a piece of music concludes with a coda, so does Dad's life.

The two most important parts of a performance are the intro and the finish. Dad's life had both. In a musical performance, people remember most how you start and how you end.

In this part of the book, I want to relay Dad's strong finish. I've had time since Dad passed to think about what words could be used to describe the man I love so much. As I mentioned at the outset of this book, our dad wasn't perfect. Multiple wonderful descriptions, however, come to mind—boundless energy, strong character, great musician, Bible scholar, Bible and music teacher, philosopher, hard worker, giving, loving, tenacious, and last, but not least, endless motivation and drive. So, it was particularly noticeable when that all began to change.

FEBRUARY 12, 2023: SUPER BOWL SUNDAY

THE GRILLED CHEESE SANDWICH

I had just spoken at a ladies' conference in Charleston, South Carolina and my plane landed in Navarre, Florida around 6 p.m. I was starving because my biological clock was still on South Carolina time, which was an hour later—7 p.m. My plan was to arrive at the house from the airport around 6:45 p.m. Florida time—and eat! On my way home from the airport, I called David, who was at a Super Bowl party with Gina. David suggested that I stop somewhere to get something to eat for Dad, Ron, and me because there wasn't much food for dinner in the house.

I decided on Arby's, but never found it. I was a tad "discombobulated" with driving home in the dark in unknown territory. My GPS couldn't keep up with the multiple turns on the back roads from the airport to home.

I tried calling Dad to make sure he was all right. He didn't answer the phone because (I later found out) he was busy in the kitchen trying to figure out what to eat. With delays finding my car, trouble exiting the airport, and getting lost driving home, I arrived home at about 8 p.m. instead of 6:45 p.m. By the time I arrived, Dad was warming up some Campbell's soup. He couldn't remember what was going on nor why he and Ron were home all alone.

David had previously jimmy-rigged Dad's computer so he and I could watch the Super Bowl on their TV. As I arrived, the TV had lost its connection. Dad was unusually upset, which made me even more so. I called David again—there was little food, no Super Bowl, a lot of tired, and Dad was distraught that he hadn't had supper. I was NOT in a good state of mind.

I told David, "You are testing the Jesus in me." He responded, "What did I do?" "You and Gina are at a party having fun and eating. I had a hard time finding my way home. There's no food for Dad, Ron, and me, Dad's upset, and the TV won't work so we can't watch the Super Bowl." David then tried to FaceTime me to get the computer connected again to the TV. No success.

David decided to leave his party and drive back home to get the Super Bowl on for us. David arrived and fixed the connection. When the game came back on, it was halftime. Dad said, "I'm not watching that junk." David by now was totally frustrated. I told him, "I'm sorry. But please don't turn the TV off. I'll never find the connection again. Just mute the halftime show so we don't miss the second half of the game."

David agreed and left to go back to his party. I returned to the kitchen. "Now," I wondered, "what to make for supper?" All I could find was bread, cheese, and butter. Of course, duh, grilled cheese. I immediately went to work making Dad, Ron, and me grilled cheese sandwiches. (It was now at least 8:45 p.m. Florida time, but my hungry stomach thought it was 9:45 p.m. Charleston time.)

Gina's three dogs started barking. I gave them all that was left of the dog food, which was gone in a flash. I then gave Dad and Ron their grilled cheese sandwiches. Dad informed me, "I'd better only eat half. Cheese and I don't always agree." The dogs kept barking because they were still hungry. So, I made them scrambled eggs.

I finally sat down to watch the game. Gina texted me, "I'm so sorry." I texted back, "No problem. I'm eating all your chocolates I found on the kitchen island." Sadly, I was. Dad finished half of the sandwich and said, "That tasted so good. I really shouldn't, but I'm going to eat the second half."

After the Super Bowl, the three of us went to bed. Gina and David arrived sometime after we were already asleep. All seemed well. I, however, was completely exhausted.

DAY 1: MONDAY, FEBRUARY 13, 2023

The next morning, all was not well. Dad was not well. Unknown to us, it was Day 1 of Dad's short-goodbye illness.

The day after Dad ate the grilled cheese sandwich, Dad had a great deal of stomach pain. He stayed most of the day in bed or in the living room leather chair. David, Gina, and I talked about sending Dad to the ER the next morning, on Tuesday, if he wasn't any better.

DAY 2: **TUESDAY, FEBRUARY 14, 2023 (VALENTINE'S DAY)**

The next morning came and went. Dad hurt so much, he didn't want to get out of bed at all and therefore slept all day. David, Gina, and I didn't want to wake him, so we agreed to wait to take him to the ER on Wednesday if he still wasn't better. Sleep might be just the thing he needed.

DAY 3: **WEDNESDAY, FEBRUARY 15, 2023**

Wednesday morning came, and Dad, if anything, was worse. As soon as they both got dressed, Gina took Dad to an ER in Navarre. I stayed home watching over Ron. When Ron's caregiver arrived, I went to join Dad and Gina. As I entered the patient's area, I was met by the ER doctor, Dr. Bell.

I smiled to myself as Ron's eye surgeon years ago was also named Dr. Bell. Come to find out, this Dr. Bell was a Christian and had sent his son to Camp of the Pines in the Pensacola area. Dad and Mom used to do the music at this Christian camp, and I remember being a camper there. This was a special God-wink.

Dr. Bell asked me if I wanted to see Dad's CT scan. I did. On the scan was a large mass in Dad's lower abdomen which the radiologist felt was originating from Dad's prostate. Nodules were also detected in Dad's lungs. Dr. Bell had called for an ambulance to come get Dad and take him to Sacred Heart Hospital in Pensacola, Florida. He told me, "You should be prepared for a prolonged stay there." (Interestingly, once there, it took a week and a half, along with multiple tests and doctors, for the Sacred Heart Hospital to confirm Dr. Bell's original prognosis.)

Once in Dad's ER room, Gina asked me to go get Dad a smoothie since he hadn't eaten in two days. I did so. When I arrived back to the ER, I found out that Dad was already loaded up in the ambulance. I asked Regina, the driver, if I could give Dad the smoothie. She said, "Step on up. He can have one sip." Sonny, the EMT in the back with Dad asked me, "Do you want to ride along?" I replied, "Can I?" "Sure." I asked Gina who was outside the ambulance, "Is it okay if I go?" Gina replied, "Surely, if you want to."

So, off Dad and I went in the ambulance—something that wasn't on my docket for the day. Since I wasn't planning on going to the Pensacola hospital, I had not packed a thing. David and Gina followed not far behind us in their car as Dad and I rode in the ambulance to the hospital.

An hour later, we arrived at the Sacred Heart ER about 5:30 p.m. Unfortunately, the ER in Pensacola was slammed with patients. Dan, Dad's ER nurse, told us that the entire hospital had been that way since America got clearance from COVID. He guessed people had waited to take care of ailments and surgeries till they felt safe. There seemed to be a plethora of sick people and only a limited few to take care of them.

We settled in and waited and waited in the ER for a doctor to come available.

David and Gina arrived soon after.

Our good friend, Ronnie Brooks, Ron and Barbara Brook's son, stopped by for a visit. He was taking a much-needed vacation from his cancer treatments. He and his wife Lynn, were living at Lynn's parent's home in Pensacola at the time, just three miles from the hospital.

Tim Willingham, Dad's close confidant on everything, also came for a visit with his wife Jennifer. Afterwards, David Greene left to go get Gina and me some Chick Fil A.

A second shift nurse, Rachel, came in. She asked Dad (who had taken his hearing aids out), "Do you like the head of your bed raised up like this, or would you like to lay flat?" Dad looked at her, "What did you say?" Gina repeated the question a little more loudly, "She said, 'Do you want your bed raised up like this, or do you want to lay flat?'" Dad looked over at Gina, "What?" Gina spoke even more loudly and enunciated very clearly, "DO YOU WANT YOUR BED RAISED UP, OR DO YOU WANT TO LAY FLAT?" Dad responded, "Lie. Do you want to lie flat?"

Nothing wrong with Dad's brain. The nurse responded, "This is not the time for a lesson in grammar." We all smiled.

Well, it was now 9 p.m. We had eaten our Chick Fil A. Our present problem: who was going home and who was staying with Dad. My issue was that I hadn't had time to pack, specifically my sleeping pills. I could stay at the hospital with Dad but wouldn't sleep a wink. Gina said, "Good. Then, you can keep a close watch on Dad all night." We laughed. Thank you, Gina Gay.

It was finally decided, since we only had one car, David and I would drive back to Navarre and Gina would stay with Dad. Gina could sleep anywhere. Me, not so much! David had an early morning inspection scheduled, and I needed a sleeping pill. Back at home in Navarre, I slept very well. Gina, back at the hospital, unfortunately had resorted to placing a thin hospital blanket on the floor to get some much-needed rest.

DAY 4: THURSDAY, FEBRUARY 16, 2023

Thursday morning, I packed an overnight bag for myself and some needed items for Dad. As soon as Ron's caregiver arrived, I made the fifty-minute drive to the Pensacola hospital and got there at 9:30 a.m. Dad and Gina were still waiting in the ER for a hospital room to come available. I relieved Gina at the Sacred Heart Hospital, and Gina took the car to go home—our first changing of the guard for (what turned out to be) Dad's eight-day hospital stay.

While Dad and I waited in the ER, a hospital room was finally assigned, but wasn't cleaned and prepared yet. Dad was still in a lot of pain but pretty well medicated. I told him, "I'm so sorry I gave you that grilled cheese sandwich." Dad comforted me, "If it weren't for me getting sick from that sandwich, we may never have found the more serious problem. God was in it."

Late Thursday afternoon, around 5 p.m., Dad's room was finally ready—room 211 on the oncology floor. Thursday night, I spent a restless night in the hospital recliner by Dad's bed. I had developed a bad cold, but life must go on.

DAY 5: FRIDAY, FEBRUARY 17, 2023

Friday was uneventful, except for the myriad of different kinds of doctor specialists who came in and out to look at Dad. Dad still didn't want to eat. By late afternoon, Gina returned to the hospital to take her turn. I went back home to Navarre.

Back at the house, everywhere I turned I thought of Dad. The kitchen trash was full (Dad always took out the trash); I opened the kitchen cabinet for a paper plate (Dad always bought them and put them there); I went to the dishwasher and the clean dishes hadn't been emptied (Dad always put the clean dishes away). I was talking to Ron in his hospice bed, and I heard a back door open. I looked, thinking it was Dad, but alas, he wasn't there. My heart ached as I remembered he was sick in the hospital. Fortunately, that night I slept very well now that I was back home in Navarre.

DAY 6: SATURDAY, FEBRUARY 18, 2023

I woke up Saturday morning semi-refreshed. By the afternoon, it was time for me to return to the hospital for another changing of the guard. Gina met me at the Emergency Room entrance. This had become our meeting spot to switch places. I got out of the car, and Gina got in.

Gina informed me that she could tell that Dad was feeling better because he was becoming more demanding: "Gina, get me a Kleenex. I need some more ice water. Get me my bathrobe so I'm more decent. I need some Blistex." Gina told me, "You and Dad are like two peas in a pod. King and Queen of the mountain. 'I need this or that, and I need it now!'" I replied, "Gina, I'm afraid you are right." Yikes. "But Dad and I are so loveable. Right?" Well, Dad was. I didn't know about me.

Gina took off to Navarre in the car. Me—I took the well-known trek, walking through the emergency room and back up to Dad's hospital room.

When I got to his room I told him, "Gina knows you are feeling better because you've become more demanding. She says we are two peas in a pod. We both want things done *now*." Dad replied, "I don't want things done now. I want them done *yesterday*."

Dad had a sweet nurse that day named Jacqueline. He quoted her parts of the book of Revelation that he had memorized. In the past couple of months, Dad had memorized the first three chapters of Revelation as well as the last four. In retrospect, I believe God led Dad to memorize Scripture on heaven, having foreknowledge for where Dad would soon be going.

After Dad quoted some of the book of Revelation to Jacqueline, she told me, "Can I please be him when I'm ninety-two?"

I was supposed to fly out that coming Wednesday to speak at a ladies' conference in Napa Valley. I had been waiting to see how Dad's situation panned out before deciding whether to go or not. I had texted Pastor Mike Ray of Hopewell Baptist Church the day before to start the conversation. Now, I was just waiting to figure it all out.

I was still under the weather with a cold. When it rained, it poured. Our dear friend, Ronnie Brooks, had volunteered to spend the night in the hospital reclining chair by Dad's bed. I was very willing to accept his kind offer because Gina and I didn't want to leave Dad alone. So, Ronnie came to relieve me in Dad's hospital room Saturday evening. Ray and Ann Gibbs had offered me the apartment at their house Ray built for Grandma B. I accepted that as well. Ann Gibbs came and picked me up, and I went there to sleep so I could get over my cold faster.

DAY 7: SUNDAY, FEBRUARY 19, 2023

Sunday morning came without fanfare. Ray and Ann took me back to the hospital before choir practice Sunday morning to relieve Ronnie Brooks. Ron's and my son Jason is Ann's choir director at Northstone Baptist Church. They figured he'd understand if Ann was late.

No gathering together with fellow believers for Dad and me. No lifting our voices in song to worship. But in our hearts, Jesus' presence was very real. He saw us. He knew our situation. He cared.

Gettys Allen visited Dad in the afternoon. They both had honorary doctorate degrees and had used them to their advantage. When visiting hospital patients and not being allowed in, they had emphasized the prefix to their names, "I'm DOCTOR Frank Garlock" or "I'm DOCTOR Gettys Allen." (No need to explain what kind of doctor, right?) Hospital staff, "Yes, Sir. Come on back."

Ronnie Brooks returned to visit. Ronnie had visited Dad every day. He always brought treats and coffee, if requested. He gave me his phone number and said, "You call me for anything, and I mean ANYTHING."

Dad had been complaining, "I don't know why the hospital buys such cheap Kleenex. They make my nose sore. They should have the soft three-ply Kleenix I buy." I said, "Dad, it's because they buy expensive MRI machines and biopsy machines. That's where they put their money. They put their money where their mouth is, and that's where you want their money to go."

So, when Ronnie asked what he could do, I told him about the three-ply Kleenex. He immediately went and bought some. I now laughingly call him, "Three-ply Ronnie."

Dad rested for a while. When he awoke, he told me that the lyrics for the song he wrote, "Speak Lord, in the Stillness" had been circling in his head since he got sick. He sang them to me:

**Speak, Lord, in the stillness; Speak, dear Lord to me.
Hush my heart to listen; Keep my thoughts on thee.
How I need Thy presence; How I need Thy care.
Speak, Lord, in the stillness, As I kneel in prayer.**

Calm the storms within me; Drive away the fears.
Quiet ev'ry murmur; Wash away my tears.
How I need Thy wisdom; How I need Thy pow'r.
Teach me, Lord, to listen in the quiet hour.
Help me trust Thy goodness; Let me know Thy will.
Fill me with Thy Spirit; Keep me calm and still.
May I trust Thee fully; Make my faith increase.
Keep my heart forever in Thy perfect, perfect peace.

Gina arrived back at the hospital late Sunday afternoon. We switched like a well-trained marching band, with precision like clockwork. We knew the drill.

DAY 8: MONDAY, FEBRUARY 20, 2023

Dad's body was so weak. All he had eaten was Jell-O and applesauce since he first showed signs of sickness a week ago, Monday, February 13. He, of course, had an IV hooked up in his arm with fluids and nutrients to keep him hydrated. Dad hurt all over, especially when he moved and especially in his lower back. His lungs were rattling with pneumonia.

Because of where Dad's pain was located, the hospital doctor told us that the prostate cancer could possibly have gone to his lungs and the bones in his lower spine. At this point, however, the urologist was telling us that the cancer could be treated and that Dad should have more time left for us to enjoy him. He had just "scraped" Dad's prostate last year at this time—whatever that meant. He was certain the cancer couldn't be far advanced.

While home, I got a call from Pastor Mike Rae of Nappa Valley. He told me I was in no way supposed to leave my dad and fly to the conference. I only had one dad, and he needed me. I felt so relieved to not leave him.

Late afternoon, I began the drive to the hospital in my car. Getting to the Ascension Sacred Heart Hospital in Pensacola from Navarre was a piece of cake. There were only two turns for the fifty-minute drive—right up my directionally-challenged brain's alley. I took a left from David and Gina's street onto Highway 98, drove forty minutes, crossed the new bridge into Pensacola, turned right onto 9th Street and, ten minutes later—*voila!* There stood the beautiful hospital straight and tall like a regal lady reaching her arms into the sky with hope and comfort.

When I arrived, I parked the car and went directly up to the second floor, room 211. When I saw my daddy, his body was weak but as usual, his spirits, good. Gina and I discussed his situation for a while. I then realized I had unfortunately forgotten my sleeping pills. And I was so exhausted from all the worrying about Dad's situation and all the comings and goings of visitors. Gina told me, "No problem. I can stay another night. I am sleeping well in the recliner."

So, I returned home to Navarre. I felt horrible that Gina had to pull a double-night duty.

DAY 9: TUESDAY, FEBRUARY 21, 2023

Tuesday morning, I drove back to the Pensacola hospital as soon as I could to relieve Gina. We made the switch.

Back in Dad's room 211, Dad and I waited for test results from two different biopsies taken the previous day. The doctors were still unsure of what type of cancer Dad had.

As Dad was in the hospital bed and I sat by him quietly, he suddenly blurted out, "I believe in the hereafter." Silence. "I go into a room and wonder what I'm here after." Oh, Daddy. You were still making me laugh.

Dad got a shot of calcium in the morning, and we waited three hours for it to make its way into Dad's bones. At 2 p.m., Dad went for a bone scan.

Dad's mouth, lips, tongue, and nose were swollen with painful sores. Have I yet said that Dad's back teeth dentures had gone missing on Sunday at the hospital? Lovely! We looked through the trash. The hospital kitchen staff looked through the second-floor hospital meal trays. No luck! Very fortunately, he was still on a soft food diet.

Gina called me. She wanted to know if I would mind staying at the hospital Tuesday night and Wednesday so she could get the house ready for her kids who were coming from the ends of the United States. Many were already on their way to visit Dad. Of course, I didn't mind.

Ron's and my son Jason and his wife Stephanie had been coming to visit every evening after their workday. Dad said they were like rays of sunshine in his day. Tuesday evening, after they left, I turned on Fox News. Dad's eyes were closed, so I was unaware that he was paying attention. The news was about the train derailment in Palestine, Ohio.

Dad perked up. "Philip Bliss, writer of the music for 'It Is Well with My Soul' died in a trainwreck in Ohio. I wonder if it was close to this recent trainwreck?" I looked it up on my computer. "Well, Dad, you are right. Philip Bliss died in a train disaster in 1876 over the Ashtabula River, seventy miles from Palestine."

Dad teared up. "Bliss was able to escape the train wreckage alive, but soon realized his wife had not. He went back into their train car that was on fire so that she wouldn't have to die alone." In the foreword of this book, I mentioned Dad's memory was iron-clad. All of us, his close relatives, were constantly astonished.

These days spent with Dad were later to be held close to my heart. Memories abounded as I sat alone with Dad. Life had come to a standstill. Dad and I were forced to stop from our busy activities to be quiet and enjoy each other's company. Dad slept much of the time, allowing me to think of pleasant times.

When presented with the possibility of losing my dad, my mind was amazingly flooded with fond memories of him. I remembered Dad sitting with me at one of my kid's soccer games. (I am normally of a quiet temperament—my children don't believe me. However, at soccer games, I totally come out of myself.) I was screaming at one of those games for our team to make a score. Dad turned to the people sitting on the other side of me and said, "A voice—soft, gentle, and low—an excellent thing in a woman."

I also remembered the time when Dad took me up north to a meeting with him in his little Volkswagen. I was about thirteen years old. A friend of ours from Dad's church choir, Juanita Learn, went with us to visit some of her family. About a mile out from an interstate exit, the BMW broke down. There we sat, in the sweltering summer heat, wondering what to do. (You must remember, there were no cell phones at the time.)

Dad decided to leave Miss Learn and me in the car, while he walked up the side of the interstate to the closest exit to get help. Dad called Mom as soon as he saw a telephone. He had been brave until that moment, but when he heard Mom's voice, he broke down. Dad finally found someone to take him to come get Miss Learn and me. Once at the gas station, I was never more grateful to find a restroom.

I also reminisced about when I was little, always telling Dad that I wanted to marry him when I grew up. This had culminated in him writing me a song, "I Want to Marry Daddy When I Grow Up."

The beeping of the machines and other hospital noises brought me back to the present reality of sitting by Dad's side in the hospital room. Dad would have two biopsies later today. The doctor told us that after that, we would be put in the oncologist's hands and given our options.

It felt so weird to be in this scenario. I remembered after I delivered each of our five babies, Dad would go get me ice cream. I could hardly wait till the hospital nutritionist allowed Dad to have ice cream. It was payback time, Dad.

But I never got that privilege.

DAY 10: **WEDNESDAY, FEBRUARY 22, 2023**

When I woke up at the hospital that morning, Dad told me, "I woke up today thinking this is going to be a special day. Today is the tenth day of my trial. I dreamed this morning of a devotional Gina had shown me recently on Proverbs 21:31: 'The horse is prepared against the day of battle: but safety is of the Lord.'"

Dad continued, "I could see the Scripture printed on the left-hand side of the book. Behind the page with the Scripture was another page of Scripture. Reading it to me was the voice of an angel. The angel started quoting Psalm 91. 'He that dwelleth in the secret place of the most High shall abide under the shadow of the Almighty.' The angel continued, 'You are in God's hands. Today is going to be a special day because you are special to the Lord.' I have always been aware of God's leading in my life. I, however, am not anything special. Why would God take notice of me?"

After his question, he assured himself; "I do know there are no mistakes. God brought Dr. Plunkett into my life two years ago to do my prostate procedures. Dr. Plunkett is a strong Christian. God brought me here to this hospital, right where Dr. Plunkett is. Gina wanted to go to a different hospital that was closer. But God brought us here. Dr. Plunkett is an expert and does five prostate operations a day. He does it for the Lord and loves what he does. God's timing is always right."

Dad kept going, "You get to be here with me through this time because God directed you to bring Ron to live with us in Navarre. Also, one of my male nurses here, Oliver, is a graduate of PCC and loves the Lord. Oliver is from Albany, NY where my brother Vic lives. I see God's leading everywhere."

Dad then asked me, "Have you ever seen the movie about the famous horse Secretariat? No one took note of him except one little girl—Penny Chenery. She took an interest in him when nobody else wanted him. She loved that horse so much and had a special relationship with him.

"The other family members thought she was spending too much money on the horse, but she believed in that horse. She trusted a jockey whom no one else wanted. The jockey was thought to be pushing the horse too hard, but she said, 'He knows the horse. Let him do what he will.' Secretariat came to be the first triple crown winner in twenty-five years."

Dad continued thoughtfully, "Penny believed in the horse when no one else did. That's what God did for me. He took note of a small boy from an unknown town in New Jersey who was one of nine children. God sent me an angel this morning to let me know that He sees me and will take care of me. I am at peace."

That Wednesday was an extra special day being with my dad. I'm so thankful God saw fit to allow me to be with him at this time. "God never moves without purpose or plan."

After Dad's moving words, he went back to resting, and I went to get myself a coffee at the hospital Starbucks. I was not gone long. But when I came back to the room, Dad informed me that three different doctors had come and gone. Dad couldn't hear much without his hearing aids and was confused as to what they said. I was extremely upset because I had been waiting for hours to speak to these doctors.

Soon after, Pastor Josh Burdick, the care pastor from Pensacola Campus Church, came to visit and pray with us. He was very kind and encouraging.

At about 1:30 p.m., an oncologist came in. Her name was Chanci. I told her that I had missed seeing the first three doctors that morning. Chanci saw how upset I was. She was so sweet and understanding. She took the time to show me Dad's computer charts where we could read all the doctors' notes—the oncologist, urologist, infectious disease doctor, pulmonologist, hospital doctor, and other practitioners.

As we reviewed the notes, Chanci told me, "So, what we do know is that your dad has stage 4 cancer." "What? That's the first time I've heard these words." She responded, "Yes, it's metastasized in his bones and lungs and is aggressive. His prostate numbers have gone from just 14 (which is high) to 140 just this week here at the hospital."

With this new news, I broke down and cried. She gave me a hug and took me out into the hall to finish our conversation. That was the first time that the words "stage 4" and "aggressive" had been spoken aloud. She continued, "Where his cancer has spread will be very hard to treat." I told her, "Dad, David, Gina, and I had already talked about not wanting any chemo or radiation." She replied, "That's totally reasonable. The treatments are not pleasant. Without them, he may have a month left."

I asked Chanci, "I know you can't say for sure, but with your experience, what is your best guess as to how much time Dad has left without treatments?" Chanci responded, "In reality, a week or two."

I was in shock. After my conversation with Chanci, I called Gina, Randy, David, my children, and a few close friends. Our family knew we would lose Ron in the not-so-distant future due to his dementia, but we never guessed Daddy would go first. We all thought Dad, as strong and clear-minded as he was, would live to be one hundred. We were all in shock. When I FaceTimed my daughter, Megs on the phone, she started crying. Hamilton and Ella, her children, looked at her confused; "What's wrong, Mommy?" Megs said, "I don't think they've ever seen me cry before." She was probably right. Megs hardly ever cried.

When I went back into Dad's room after calling family and close friends, Dr. Plunkett the urologist came in to visit. He confirmed all that the oncologist had just told me. After he left, I could not stop sobbing. Gina and David weren't with me. I wished somebody would be. Dad woke up and looked at me. I thought to myself, "I've got to tell him. It's not right that the whole family knows, and Dad doesn't. It's HIS body."

In Dad's room, I faced him all alone. All alone, except for God. I still felt the heavy weight and grief. I went to Dad's bedside, leaned over him, and began very slowly and carefully. "Dad, we don't have good news. . . . "

I finished as bravely as I could with what I knew. Dad teared up and said, "But I had such peace this morning. I thought for sure God was going to give me three more years." I replied with tears streaming down my cheeks, "God did give you a peace. It is a peace to carry you through to your finish line. Dad, you have fought a good fight. You have kept the faith. You are going to see Jesus whom you have served all these years. You are going to see Mom and Jonathan." Dad was crying hard now as well, but managed to get the words out, "I still have peace. I have always been aware of God's leading in my life. I, however, have such mixed emotions. I want to see my Lord but don't want to leave my family behind."

I so wish someone had been with Dad and me. Then suddenly, my phone rang. It was Pastor Jeff Redlin, a close family friend for many years now and someone whom Dad loved very much. I had previously texted him our recent news, but he hadn't seen it yet. He had been out visiting with his associate, Pastor Josh, and thought, "I should call Shelly." Dad, Gina, and I watched Pastor Jeff preach on TV almost every Sunday. His call was a welcome boost of encouragement and comfort from the Lord. He then prayed with us.

After our call with Pastor Jeff was over, Dad assured me, "I truly am at peace. I am so thankful that God brought you and Ron along and now Adam and Megan to continue the music ministry God burdened me with fifty years ago. Did you know that it gives me more joy to see Adam and Megan running and writing the music for Majesty Music than if I were doing it myself?"

I called Gina, "I need you here with Dad and me." She and David promised to come immediately.

\\\\\\\\\\\\\

As Dad fell asleep, I thought of another fun time spent with Dad. Dad and I were painting the front of our home on the back campus of Bob Jones University. We donned it with buttery lemon coats of fresh yellow paint, Mom's favorite color. As we worked, Dad and I made up a song. It's the only one I can ever remember us writing together. I mentioned it to Dad after he woke up as we were still encamping together in the hospital room. We immediately broke out into song. The chorus went:

Goof 'em up Charlie, that's my name.
Goof 'em up Charlie, what a shame.
Goof 'em up Charlie, I'm to blame.
Goof 'em up Charlie, that's my name."

Stanza 1
I took my girl on a date one night.
The dress she wore was oh, so tight.
The fellas got fresh, and we had a fight.
I got punched, and what a sight.

\\\\\\\\\\\\\

Gina and David arrived. The three of us spoke to Dad about his recent prognosis. We all agreed again—no treatments. Was pain and discomfort a reason to extend his life a month or two? Gina and David left to drive back home to Navarre. I stayed at the hospital with Dad.

DAY 11: **THURSDAY, FEBRUARY 23, 2023**

Thursday, the day after we found out Dad's sad prognosis the visitors began to pour in. First, our sweet Torie, David and Gina's daughter, drove the five-hour trip from Birmingham, Alabama to Pensacola. Torie was an ICU nurse and had come to help us take care of Dad in the hospital.

Torie arrived early in the morning. She walked into Daddy's room already knowing our sad news. With a smile on her face, she asked Dad, "Pop-Pop, are you so excited you get to go see Jesus?" She continued, "You're going to be able to prove right what you've studied all these years. And you get to see Nana."

Dad, Torie, his nurse Kella who graduated from PCC, and I all started to cry. They were tears of joy as well as sorrow.

Dad still hadn't eaten anything but a few bites of Jell-O, and he didn't want to drink. Torie told him, "The less you eat, the faster you're going to die." Dad complied, "Ok. I'll eat this yogurt." Torie later explained to me, "You've got to be honest with someone who knows they are going to soon die. They know what's going on. There is no need to beat around the bush." I knew she was right, because she had dealt with this numerous times. Although this time, it was her Pop-Pop.

In the afternoon, our friend Gettys Allen brought Dr. Arlin Horton, founder of Pensacola Christian College, to visit. As

I've explained, Mom and Dad had come to Pensacola in 1954, three months after I was born in Rochester, New York. The church where Dad had ministered was located on the property of PCC. During this three-year time frame of Dad's ministry (1954-1957) my parents became fast and close friends with Arlin and Beka.

Uncle Arlin, as Randy, Gina, and I called him, started Pensacola Elementary School. Uncle Arlin eventually bought fifty surrounding properties to develop into what is now known as the campus of PCC. Aunt Beka, as we called her, had a TV program where she used flannel graph to tell Bible stories to children. In fact, when I was three years old, I had the privilege to sing a solo on Aunt Beka's program.

Uncle Arlin Horton is a phenomenal businessman. As he was visiting Dad with Gettys Allen, they all had stories to tell. While we gathered round Dad's bed, Gina asked Uncle Arlin if he could remember a story about Dad. As he was thinking, Dad interjected, "I have one to tell." Dad remembered when Uncle Arlin, Aunt Beka, he, and Mom went on an overnight stay at the Holiday Inn on Highway 98 in Destin. At the time, the road was only two lanes, and the Holiday Inn was uniquely circular and about the only building in Destin. On top of the hotel was a rotating restaurant.

Well, as the story went, the two couples had both forgotten their toothpaste. Arlin and Dad went across the street to a small drugstore. Apparently, Uncle Arlin tried to get the store clerk to sell him two tubes of toothpaste for the price of one.

Once a businessman, always a businessman.

Next, Cleusia and Pitagorus Goncalves came to the hospital to visit. Dad loved Cleusia, the Pensacola Christian College and Pensacola Campus Church choir director. He thought she was the best choral director he'd ever seen. The two of them had gotten very close over the last five years. He told Cleusia that he wanted her to have one of his favorite choral director books from his library. (As sick as Dad was, his mind was still clear and working overtime.)

Pastor Jeff Redlin came next, sat down by Dad's bedside, and gave us a ten-minute devotional God had laid on his heart. Then Evangelist Mike Manor, who was preaching that week in Panama City, followed. Mike had been a lifetime friend and written some of the Patch the Pirate songs used on the adventure recordings. Mike had stopped at David and Gina's house first to visit Ron before coming to see Dad. It was a full day.

Our family shed multiple tears since our news the day before. Today, Gina's other four kids with their families were en route to Florida. Gina had spent the afternoon at home in Navarre, washing sheets, cleaning, and preparing for their arrival. I had consequently spent Tuesday, Tuesday night, Wednesday, Wednesday night, and Thursday with Dad—precious, precious time.

There was light at the end of the tunnel. And that light was glorious!

That light is available to all. That light is bright and full of color unimaginable to our naked eye. That light is heaven. That light is Jesus.

DAY 12: **FRIDAY, FEBRUARY 24, 2023**

I am still staying with Dad, as Gina has a house full of family. I felt honored to spend this precious time with my sweet daddy. My heart was so full of emotion and my head was swimming in thought.

The first couple of days since learning Dad's diagnosis had passed by ever so slowly, like a ticking time bomb waiting to explode. Each minute, however, had been and continued to be special with Dad.

That day, Dad told me, "Shelly, you are such a good writer. And a good speaker." I replied, "Well, Dad, I am like you, but without the stamina and smarts. But I'll take what I can get."

By that evening, most members of Gina and David's family converged on Sacred Heart Hospital. The time was spent in a glorious reunion, sharing memories and reasons why they all loved Dad. A nurse's aide stopped me in the hallway after they left and said, "You have a beautiful family." I admitted, "Well, they aren't my kids, but thank you. I'll claim them."

At the end of the evening, Dad's nurse Kella, who was a graduate of PCC came into Dad's hospital room. She said, "My mom from Texas just texted me and said, 'I just saw you on Shelly's Facebook page. Are you Dr. Garlock's nurse?'" Smiles.

All Dad's nurses and aides loved him. In fact, one told me that when nursing shifts changed, they would tell each other, "You are going to love the gentleman in room 211."

God continued to work on my dad's behalf: the Sacred Heart Hospital doctor on call the last few days had been Dr. Hof. When I told Dr. Hof a day ago that our family had decided we did not want to put Dad through chemo or radiation, he recommended, "Let's put your dad directly into hospice care." Agreed. Gina and I wanted Dad to be comfortable at home in our presence when it was time to go to his final home in heaven.

Come to find out, Dr. Hof was on the medical board of Genteva, formerly Regency Care, the same hospice group my Ron had been on for five years. (Hospice would not take you unless they thought you had under two years left to live, yet Ron had beaten the odds and was still here.)

Fortunately, Dad could use the same hospice nurses, aides, social workers, and other personnel that were already coming to the house for Ron. Even Charlie, Ron's hospice chaplain, would be the same. Charlie and Dad had a special connection since the first time Charlie came to visit Ron. Both were raised in New Jersey. They knew some of the same towns, churches, and people. They both had been involved in the same Youth for Christ group. We were so happy Charlie could be here for Dad as well as Ron—another sign of God's goodness.

DAYS 13 AND 14: **SATURDAY, SUNDAY, FEBRUARY 25 & 26, 2023**

On Saturday, we were able to bring Dad back home to Navarre. Everyone was exhausted. Torie decided to go back to Mobile to work her three-day shift at the hospital there. Torie believed Dad probably had about a week left. She planned to come back to help us in the end. Randy came from Greenville with his friend Beverly to see Dad. Randy's birthday was on the 27th of February, and we all prayed Dad wouldn't pass that day.

DAY 15: **MONDAY, FEBRUARY 27, 2023**

On this day, time especially seemed at a standstill. Days were again passing in slow motion as we knew the outcome of Dad's cancer was approaching soon. At night, I didn't want the next day to come because of what it might bring. I was perfectly happy in the presence of both my husband and my father.

I, however, told Dad, "Don't feel bad about leaving us. You are going to see Flora Jean, the love of your life. You've been the backbone of our family, but it's time we learn to stand on our own two feet."

Very fortunately, Dad did not pass on this day, as it was Randy's birthday after all.

DAY 16: **TUESDAY, FEBRUARY 28, 2023**

Aunt Barbara Brooks and my sweet Megan had driven down to Florida to visit with us. Our beloved Tara flew in to join them. We had a blessed time with Dad. Aunt Barbara made us laugh with stories of her, Uncle Ron, Mom, and Dad. God had indeed blessed us with enough time to share sweet memories and let Dad know how much he was loved.

We played some of Dad's music that he had written. A special one we heard over and over, "Jesus Is Lord," was played by a trombone trio with Frank Garlock, Jason Hamilton, and Ron Hamilton. Praise God.

DAY 17: **WEDNESDAY, MARCH 1, 2023**

Over the last few days, people had been asking Gina what Dad's last words of advice would be. On this day, Gina put her phone up to Dad as he lay in his hospice bed and asked him what words he would like to share with our friends who were following his journey. Without hesitation Dad said, "Give it to God." He continued, "Give your talents, your time, your money, everything you have."

This advice was no surprise to me. A few weeks back, before Dad was showing symptoms of cancer, I had been attempting to give advice to one of Ron's caregivers. Dad walked by as we were discussing the problem and simply said, "Can I tell you the best advice I know? Give it to God." He then added, "And see what amazing things God does."

On Wednesday morning, Ben Everson and his wife Amanda made a visit to see Dad. Unfortunately, Dad did not wake up.

On Wednesday afternoon, Pastor Jeff Redlin and his videographer Josh Burdick came to visit Dad. This was the first free time Pastor Jeff had since Dad had come home from the hospital to make the drive to Navarre. If Dad was up to it, he was hoping to video Dad saying a few words of encouragement for the members of Pensacola Christian Church.

Dad had not been feeling well, but when the two pastors arrived, Dad perked up. He said to Josh, "I remember you. You videotaped me several years ago, on such and such a date." Dad did an unbelievably wonderful job at the taped interview that afternoon.

DAY 18: **THURSDAY, MARCH 2, 2023**

Thursday morning, in retrospect, was to be exactly twenty-four hours before Dad passed. Early that morning, a male figure appeared at our front door. It was none other than David Price, the son of Dolphus Price, former pastor at Brent Baptist in Pensacola.

You may remember that Pastor Price was the man for whom Dad served under as music director and youth pastor sixty-nine years ago. Dad had a rough morning until David arrived. When he saw David enter his room, he amazingly rose to the occasion. The two of them had a great visit. David told Dad, "I know when you see my mom and dad in heaven, they will ask you if I came to visit. I don't want them disappointed in me before I even get there." We had a good laugh at his guilty admission.

David Price had driven eight hours just to come see Dad. Mike Herbster had done the same two days before. Dad had been a friend to top all friends. Dad had hundreds of names with their pictures on his phone for whom he prayed regularly.

Dad had loved people and sincerely poured his life into theirs. Through all of the phone calls, letters, and visits, we discovered in the last few weeks the many who sincerely loved him in return.

I was able to talk on the phone to Uncle Don, one of Dad's two surviving siblings (of the nine). He told me of visiting Franklin Road Baptist Church that past Sunday. As he sat in Sunday School, he received a tap on his shoulder. When he turned around, a lady asked, "Are you Frank Garlock's brother?" Uncle Don replied, "Yes." She continued, "Your brother led me to Christ." That was just one of many such stories we heard during this time.

That evening, David Greene tried to get home from work quickly after we had notified him that Dad was failing fast. His car's water hose burst en route on the busy US 98. As he pulled his car over to the side of the road, the auto repair shop he always used was just in line of his vision. Thankfully, David was able to walk there to get help. Another of Satan's arrows was deflected.

In the evening hours, Gina and I were by Dad's bedside. Gina was rubbing his forehead and giving him ice to quench his parched throat. I had my hand on his chest. Suddenly, Dad pointed up to the ceiling. Gina asked, "Dad, do you want the ceiling fan turned off?" He had never liked it on but was so feverish, we had it going. Dad did not respond. Thoughtfully, I asked him, "Daddy, do you see heaven?" No response. "Daddy, do you see angels?" He nodded yes. "Daddy, do you see

Jesus?" Again, he nodded yes. Chill bumps went down my spine.

Later that same evening, when Gina was out of the room, Dad pointed up to the ceiling again. "Daddy, do you see heaven?" No response. "Daddy, do you see angels?" Again, he nodded yes. "Daddy, do you see Jesus?" Like before, he nodded yes. What a sweet confirmation God gave us as to where Dad was soon to be.

It seemed so strange that Dad appeared so healthy until about three weeks ago.

DAY 19: FRIDAY, MARCH 3, 2023

It was 8 a.m. Gina, David, Reagan, Torie, the hospice nurse Kaitlyn, and I were gathered around Dad in his room. His breathing was getting more and more labored. It wouldn't be long now before Daddy's last exhale of earthly air would be followed by an inhale of celestial air.

That morning, on March 3, Kaitlyn, the hospice nurse, texted Charlie Arbertell, the hospice chaplain I mentioned earlier. She informed him that Dad was going to soon be passing. Charlie was very concerned about Dad and had been keeping up with Dad's illness by texts, even when off work. He was not scheduled to come that day, nor was it part of his hospice responsibility. But because of his love for Dad, he came. At about 10:30 a.m., when David greeted him at the door, Charlie had tears in his eyes.

Charlie, on one of his prior visits, recalled to me the time he first met Dad. Apparently, the subject of Bob Jones University had come up. During the conversation, Charlie told Dad, "I read a book once called *Pop Goes the Gospel* by a Frank Garlock." Dad paused for a few seconds. Then pointing to himself, he said, "I'm Frank Garlock." Charlie, surprised, responded, "What? No way." Dad, pleased at the connection, confirmed, "Yes. I'm Frank Garlock." Charlie looked like a deer caught in headlights. They had a lot to talk about.

At the time of Charlie's visit, Dad was unresponsive and failing fast. The rest of the family was keeping busy in other parts of the house. Gina had Christian music playing in the living room within listening distance of Dad's bed.

I was sitting in Dad's room holding his hands. After Charlie entered, he read some Scripture to us. Charlie and I visited as Dad, lying in his hospice bed, was breathing haltingly and irregularly. Charlie told me, "I'd like to tell you a story that I never told your dad." I leaned forward in my chair. My interest peaked.

Charlie proceeded, "I got saved due to the Jesus Revolution in the late 1960s, early '70s. Before I became a youth pastor in New Jersey, I was a disc jockey for a Christian rock station in New York." I followed along, "Okay, this is interesting." Charlie explained, "I had a friend who was the editor for the magazine *Christian Herald*. This friend asked me to write an article for the magazine in defense of Christian rock. I did so. It was published as a two-page spread on an edition on which Amy Grant's picture donned the cover."

"Wow," I exclaimed, my mind full of questions. "About three weeks later," Charlie continued, "Bob Jones University called me. They were interested in doing a debate on their radio station with Frank Garlock." By now I was laughing and staring in disbelief: "Did you do the debate?" "Oh, yes," he replied. "I actually thought I won it." I responded, "I bet Dad thought he won." Charlie concurred, "I'm sure he did, but the call-ins after the debate crucified me. There was one in particular that I'll never forget. . . ."

Following that statement, Dad took his final breath. The time: 11:30 a.m.

As I ran to get Gina and David, I heard the song "Finally Home" begin to play on YouTube in his room. That was totally a God-thing. You couldn't convince me God or Dad's guardian angel wasn't a part of it.

David, Gina, Torie, and Reagan ran into Dad's room. I stayed in the living room, wailing. That was the second time I remember wailing—the first was after learning that Ron's and my son Jonathan had died, and the second, now after Dad's passing. I remembered crying softly right before Mom passed as I was lying by her side on her bed, but not wailing.

After I gained my composure, I went back into Dad's room to be with the family. Charlie was still there. After some time passed, I told David and Gina, "You must hear the story Charlie just told me. It's unbelievable."

Charlie retold the story about the rock music debate. Following it I asked, "What was the call-in you'll never forget?" Charlie admitted, "It was from a Southern country gentleman. He told me for all the listening radio land to hear, 'Charlie, I believe you are sincere about thinking Christian rock helps win the lost. But whenever I hear it, it makes me think I'm in the back of my pickup truck with my girlfriend. . . . '" (I won't finish the call-in comment.) Charlie asked, "How do you respond to that? I had no words."

As I walked Charlie out for him to leave, he apologized, "I'm sorry I told you about the radio debate. I didn't tell your dad because I thought I'd lose credibility as his hospice chaplain." I replied, "How I wish you had shared it with Dad. He would have thought it was hilarious. Who knows? Perhaps in Dad's final hour, he did hear it."

I had to convince Charlie that his funny story was indeed appropriate—even good—for the tragic time. Our family's humor and his seemed to be the same. Because of all the tragedy our family had endured, we had learned to find humor in everything possible. Perhaps it was a coping mechanism, or perhaps it was continuing Dad's legacy of always seeing the humor and the fun in every situation.

Charlie then told me, "I knew I shouldn't have told you the story about the rock music debate. I killed your dad." We both laughed because we knew it was ridiculous. "Charlie! At least you didn't make the grilled cheese sandwich that sent him to the ER."

Upon reflection, I now know why Charlie was in such shock when he found out months before that

the grey-headed man he was becoming friends with was Frank Garlock. Only God could have put these two back together again. The odds. God certainly has a sense of humor and brings loose ends of life together, which I call God-winks.

After Charlie left, I returned to Dad's room to be with my family who was surrounding him.

Our hearts were quiet. We committed our sweet daddy into Jesus' loving care.

SATURDAY, MARCH 4, 2023

Each time, the day after I lost someone dear to me, my brain was in a fog and my emotions spent. Mostly, my heart ached. I had done this before.

Yet, I felt amazed and overwhelmed at the same time. I was privileged to spend the last eight months in my father's presence, just as my father was now enjoying his Father's presence. Obvious to me was that God led me.

As questions were mounting about Dad's funeral and conversations were had about how Ron would be cared for while we were gone, words from my father consoled my heart: "Give it to God."

I had, at times, kicked myself for buying a camper. Doing so had caused my sweet brother-in-law, David Greene, all kinds of extra work, and I now had debt. What would Ron have done? But now it seemed obvious that God had led me. Only He could have known we would need extra sleeping quarters these past two weeks. Also, Alyssa had just found out that she had Covid. Thankfully, because of the camper, she could effectively quarantine. God saw us.

I called our close friend Aunt Carole Blyth on the phone to tell her of Dad's passing. She mentioned, "I bet your dad was his normal self, encouraging people, up until he started losing consciousness." Boy, was she right.

SUNDAY, MARCH 5, 2023

Since Friday, David and I had spent hours on our phones and computers planning Dad's funeral arrangements. With all of the family's schedules and locations, the timing of Dad's "Celebration of Life" service was difficult to put together. We finally came to an agreement:

Dr. Frank Garlock's funeral service would be at 4:30 p.m. on Saturday, March 11, at Faith Baptist Church (viewing directly preceding).

I had been quoting "Give it to God" multiple times to myself since Dad passed. I knew God's timing was always right. But today, a seemingly insurmountable roadblock hit us from out of nowhere. David, Gina, and I went to our knees tonight praying, "God, we give this to you."

Jason and Stephanie had also contracted Covid this week along with Alyssa. We were praying they could all come to the celebration service, and that Jason would still be able to sing. The three of them would just have enough time to complete the recommended quarantine. I mediated on Isaiah 41:13, "For I the LORD thy God will hold thy hand, saying unto thee, Fear not; I will help thee." *Fear not; I WILL help thee*. I clung to this promise.

WEDNESDAY, MARCH 8, 2023

Today was Gina's sixtieth birthday. God's timing was perfect. We prayed Dad's homegoing wouldn't be on Randy or Gina's birthdays. Praise God it occurred right in between.

I awoke at 6:45 the morning of Gina's birthday. David, Torie, Reagan, and Justin were all sitting in the living room having coffee with their momma, Gina. Whatever weaknesses our family had, being loving was not one of them.

As I looked on, I had mixed emotions: I was glad Gina would be surrounded by her children and grandchildren on her birthday, but I was disappointed I could not join in the celebration. I had to drive to Greenville to make the final funeral arrangements. I hated to miss the festivities, which because of the circumstances, would be minimal.

Gina Gay deserved to be celebrated. Gina was a born caregiver. She had always loved taking care of babies, children, and animals. Since she was a little girl, she had said she wanted to take care of Mom and Dad when they were old. It hadn't been an easy job for her and David, but sweetly, faithfully, and patiently they had accomplished something they will never regret.

Gina Gay is very much like our mom—an excellent home keeper, great cook, organizer, and nurturer of all babies and animals. Mom grew up on a farm in Oklahoma—Gina's dream. I, on the other hand, am more like Dad. I love to research, write books, write music, and teach.

Since Dad passed away four days ago, we each implemented our gifts to the tasks at hand—Gina cleaning up, cooking, and entertaining the guests and I, writing the obituary, the service program, and the bio.

Additionally, David Greene had been the main point person for everything involved with the hospital, hospice, caregivers, and mortuary. (David also had been, unfortunately for him, the only one who could take care of many of Dad's needs and mine with regards to the pool, Dad's computer, Dad's bank account, my camper, and more.) My brother, Randy Garlock, was handling Dad's health insurance details.

FRIDAY, MARCH 10, 2023

Our family was on the home stretch. We worked together to close the final chapter of Dad's good life. Randy, Gina, and my greatest desire was to give this great man, Dr. Frank Watson Garlock whom we were privileged to call Dad, proper honor. And of primary importance, we wanted to give the God he served his entire life, the glory due His name.

The phrase, "on the home stretch" originated at horse races, where the horses were nearing the finishing line. Oddly enough, the last (almost) four weeks now had seemed like a horse race. Not a long-distance race, but a harried and exhausting short sprint. And you can be certain, that while this horse had been racing, Satan had sent his principalities and powers to shoot darts at the jockey, the horse's head, the horse's body, and the horse's legs and feet.

My sweet Ronnie was being well taken care of in a Florida respite facility while we drove to Greenville, South Carolina for the funeral. The respite center called me the day after we left to inform me of his safe arrival. They said he smiled all the way as he was rolled in. His caregiver, Toni, sent me a picture last night letting me know Ron was safe, well, and sound.

"God is great, God is good, let us thank Him as we should."

SATURDAY, MARCH 12, 2023

The funeral went remarkably well. All praise goes to God.

Our doctor friend, Tom Kendall, told me Dad's service was a memorial service to top all memorial services. My heart swelled with happiness. He also told me, "You are so much like your father. I guess the nut doesn't fall far from the bush." He couldn't have given me a more cherished compliment.

Many others also expressed that Dad's service honored Dad and gave glory to God. Praise Him! That was exactly our purpose.

Randy, Gina, and I each gave a eulogy. Adam also gave a eulogy as the president of Majesty Music and grandson-in-law. (Is there such a thing?) Ben, another grandson-in-law gave a eulogy/gospel presentation.

SUNDAY, MARCH 13, 2023

On Sunday, heaven wept with us. We laid Daddy, Frank Garlock, to rest at 11:00 a.m. this day. We had a small family gathering at the Graceland East Chapel to share Scripture and memories. The service was a beautiful time of singing and testimonies from those who loved Dad most. Teardrops were falling from the sky to let us know God saw us and cared at our time of grieving.

29 DAD TAUGHT ME
HOW TO DEAL WITH DEATH

> *Be thou faithful unto death, and I will give thee a crown of life. —Revelation 2:10*

In reflecting on Dad's last months of his life, Gina and I remembered him losing weight. No problem, we thought. He was exercising more and must not have been eating as much. Dad had also been sleeping later in the mornings and taking longer naps. No problem. Dad was ninety-two years young after all. Why should he still have been getting up at 6:30 a.m. every morning to go swim for an hour? Little did we know more was going on.

Had it been tough dealing with this sudden revelation of Dad's cancer? The simple answer—"yes." Was it difficult taking care of two terminally ill loved ones, Dad and my husband Ron, at the same time? Again, the simple answer— "yes." The blessings, however, far outweighed the challenges. As it was a blessing to care for one you love so much, it was a double blessing to care for two.

Tears were on each page as I daily journaled about Dad's final days.

Was it difficult for Dad to deal with his terminal prognosis? There was no easy answer. There, of course, was sadness at first. Dad, as we had known him to deal with multiple trials before, dealt with this trial with dignity, grace, and trust in the Lord. Dealing with trials was what made him the man that he was: a man of God.

Our family can't go through anything without having a funny story, so I will end with one final humorous story.

After Dad had passed, David and our friend Samantha were at the house when a young caretaker came to get Dad's body. David greeted him at the front door and took him back into the living area where Ron was asleep on his hospice bed. Dad's body was in the back bedroom.

Samantha, David, and the young man talked for a little while. Suddenly, Ron turned over a little. The man jumped, turned white as a ghost, and his eyes got big as saucers. He exclaimed, "Oh! I think he just moved." Oops, sorry, wrong guy.

A TRUE AND "MOVING" STORY

by Louise Wright

They started out at BJU,
Moved a few times there into something new.
Then bought a home on Chipwood Lane,
But Paris Mountain caused them to move again.

"It's cold up here—let's move back down."
So, again they set out to look around
To find a house they might desire—
A place of which they would never tire.

They found a house with Jacuzzi and pool,
A lovely place that made their friends drool.
But a problem arose—what should they do?
They're paying on three houses, so must get rid of two.

The house on Chipwood did not sell,
So, they moved back there again to dwell.
What's this I see! Plans to build a house
Next door to Gina, her kids, and her spouse.

Now they'll be happy, they'll settle down here
With Gina and her family being so near.
But Gina moved and they became sad.
So, a condo they found for which they were glad.

Then to Mauldin moved Gina and her crew.
So, the Garlocks wanted to move there, too.
They bought a lot on which to build,
But friends said, "No way, you're over the hill.

"With all of your travels, your meetings, and such,
The stress of building would be too much!"
So, a house they bought, a few blocks away
From David, the kids, and Gina Gay.

I called Flora Jean to make her aware
Of a dream I had—in fact, a NIGHTMARE!
I saw packed boxes. The floor was bare.
Barb and I were helping—doing our share.

I awoke from my dream and called to be sure.
They were still on Sanderling, safe and sure.
She said, "You were close, it was Gina, not me
That's selling their house and moving you see.

They'll reside in a rental while they build on our lot.
Though we are too old—they apparently are not."
As I recall their moving, a thought comes to me
Of our home in heaven throughout eternity.

Will they be content with their home on high?
Or will they still move around in the sweet by and by?